Erika Uitz

THE LEGEND OF GOOD WOMEN

Medieval Women in Towns & Cities

Moyer Bell Limited
Mt. Kisco, New York

Endpaper
Florence, view of the town.
Woodcut, printed by Anton Koberger, Nuremberg, 1493.
In: Albert Schramm, *Der Bilderschmuck der Frühdrucke*.
Vol. XVII. Leipzig, 1934, ill. 470.

Translated from the German by Sheila Marnie

Copyright © 1988 by Edition Leipzig

Published in the United States of America in 1990 by Moyer Bell
Limited

Design: Walter Schiller

The book was originally published in the German Democratic Republic as *Die Frau in der mittelalterlichen Stadt* by Edition Leipzig.

First Edition

Library of Congress Cataloging-in-Publication Data

Uitz, Erika, 1931–
   The legend of good women: medieval women in towns & cities/Erika Uitz.
   p. cm.
     ISBN 1-55921-013-3: $19.95
     1. Women—History—Middle Ages, 500–1500. 2. Cities and towns,
Medieval—Europe. I. Title.
HQ1143.U58 1990
305.4'09'02—dc20

                     89-36573
                     CIP

Printed in the German Democratic Republic

Contents

And to the doctrine of these olde wyse,
Yeven credence, in every skilful wyse,
And trowen on these olde aproved stories
Of holinesse, of regnes, of victories,
Of love, of hate, of other sundry thinges.

Geoffrey Chaucer
from *The Legend of Good Women*

Foreword

In the twelfth century a window of freedom began to open for town-dwelling European women only to close again by the end of the fifteenth century. Erika Uitz, in her meticulous representation of medieval urban life, has recreated that all-but-forgotten moment of expanding possibilities for women. Her narrative reminds us that progress toward freedom is neither predictable nor inevitable. Liberties come and go, often propelled by forces beyond our control. Professor Uitz's tale also reminds us that lost liberties have a half-life which continues to shimmer in our imaginations. This strange luminescence goes on irradiating oppression long after freedom has died.

The medieval slogan, 'Town air makes one free', referred to the city's guarantee of freedom to those residents—male *and* female—who had lived away from a feudal estate for a year and a day without being reclaimed by a lord. In the confrontation between economic and individualistic forces unleashed in the growing urban centres and the power of the declining feudal nobility, a few, fortunate women claimed unexpected spoils for themselves. Opportunities for them grew as trade expanded and the demand for labour increased. Municipal governments began providing their increasingly valuable female workers with protection from both the sexual and financial predations of the nobility as well as from some of the financial insecurities of marriage.

Town growth and expanding trade reshaped the contours of marriage for those women lucky enough to participate in the growing economy. At the beginning of the twelfth century the only contractual marriages were among nobility and were arranged to protect the rights of male inheritance. In conditions reminiscent of American plantation slavery, men and women living under the influence of a feudal lord needed his permission to marry. If tenants married between estates, the lord losing a worker had the right to claim another. In all marriages, a woman passed from the guardianship of her father to that of her husband. This transfer was sometimes symbolized by a kick from the groom to his bride.

Towns, however, made increasing legal efforts to protect females from seduction and rape by the feudal nobility in order to protect this source of urban wealth. Towns also made somewhat less concerted efforts to protect wives' property. The most fortunate (i.e. the wealthiest) married women had, by the end of the era in discussion, property and civil rights approximating those of widows. For most women, however, marriage remained an institution designed for the comfort of males. To illustrate this point, Professor Uitz writes that widows sometimes put on nuns' habits to avoid remarriage. Others, openly exercising sexual freedom for the first time, painted and bedecked themselves to attract male admiration.

Professor Uitz does not play down the complex and sometimes contradictory forces acting on women's lives. Thus, for example, town councils encouraged prostitution as one of the methods of protecting wives against the sexual advances of the nobility, the clergy and foreigners. The town fathers sacrificed the chastity of some women to secure that of richer ones. Towns profited by the brothels' revenues, sometimes sharing them with neighbouring religious institutions. At the same time prostitutes were social outcasts, prohibited from frequenting local taverns and often forced to wear distinctive clothing.

No picture of women in the Middle Ages would be complete without a discussion of religion, and so the author sketches, deftly, the complicated and often paradoxical relationship of women to the church. She gives the historical background of the church's low opinion of women, describing movements to purify Catholicism from within and how these movements affected women. The Cathari (or Albigensians, as they were known in France) attempted to purify church practices, but excluded women from its hierarchy. The all-female Beguine movement, which began in France around 1200, offered poor women a chance to lead socially useful lives without marrying. Hitherto, daughters of the rich constituted the majority of convent inhabitants. The Beguines also gave women the final say in the goals and organisation of the movement itself. The Beguines, like the Franciscans, held poverty sacred. Some begged, performed funerals and took care of the sick while others engaged in trade or textile work to support the order. The convents were under the jurisdiction of the towns, and some members became town residents with all the rights of citizenship. The Beguine vows were fluid: women could enter and leave the order depending on their needs and desires. Overall, the reader gets a sense of the extraordinary power of the church's ideals over the hearts of a wide range of women and the strenuous and diverse attempts women made to conform to these ideals.

Perhaps the most surprising material in this informative volume concerns the economic life of medieval urban women. Professor Uitz has unearthed evidence showing women in an astounding array of occupations from spinners of gold thread to illuminators of manuscripts, from trading and banking to running inns and shops. Women in some French cities (England always remained more sexist, by comparison) formed female guilds for the production of silk and yarns. Women were brewers, laundresses, barrel- and crate makers, soap boilers, candle makers, book binders, doll painters and even, if rarely, butchers. Women worked in the metal trades and some were involved in mining and making swords, scythes and sieves. Wives often followed their husbands into crafts becoming masters—or mistresses—of apprentices in their own right. A variety of guilds had male and female members, although for membership in some, women had to prove legitimate birth and a chaste reputation. This is a theme which Professor Uitz often illustrates, i.e., that women were expected to adhere to certain 'feminine' standards of behaviour which might have little bearing on doing a job. For example, a German woman innkeeper who had badgered a well-known customer about his drinking bill had to apologize for her aggressive behaviour before the town council. Thus being a good woman could be a hindrance to good business.

We are constantly encountering the unexpected in this fascinating book. We find a portrait of Christine de Pisan (b. 1364), a Venetian who wrote books protesting the degradation of women in literature and the works of the church philosophers, as well as a text helping to restore peace in France. Then we discover the fact that some towns employed women as keepers of the keys, tax collectors, town guards, shepherds, and musicians. (Women musicians usually travelled with groups because singly they were likely to be persecuted as witches.) We are told that of 321 professions in the late thirteenth and early fourteenth centuries, women numbered in 108 and that some businesswomen undertook arduous pilgrimages on their own, crossing Europe and the Alps on horseback on their way to Rome.

Professor Uitz's account of this remote time demonstrates the persistence in women's lives of the themes of poverty, powerlessness, marital oppression and societal devaluation—as well as the liberating effects of proximity to the intellectual ferment of cities and mastery of a craft or a profession. Then as now, movements promoting certain liberties, such as the medieval commune movement to achieve political, economic and social independence for towns, tended to help promote the liberty of women. Then as now, women were most highly represented in the lower economic strata of the population. Then as now, women were often paid less for the same work men were doing. Then as now, women's work was essential in accumulating and increasing family capital.

Through the imaginative use of municipal and guild records, wills and diaries, Erika Uitz has unearthed fascinating stories from the Middle Ages. She has located these scenes in an analytic framework, thereby providing us with a colourful vision of an important episode of women's history and an oblique, thought-provoking comment of the evanescence of liberty.

Martha Saxton

A woman ruffles her husband's hair; another musters her husband's clothes.
Woodcut, printed by Günther Zainer, Augsburg, 1477.
In: Albert Schramm, *Der Bilderschmuck der Frühdrucke*. Vol. II.
Leipzig, 1920, ill. 711.

Introduction

* How did independent women earn and use their money and possessions in medieval western and central Europe, and particularly in Germany? What kinds of partnerships did working wives form with their husbands? How great or little control were widows permitted over the family business? What position did females occupy in guilds and trade unions? In short, how did women make a living during the Middle Ages?

Between the twelfth and sixteenth centuries, an almost total transformation occurred in urban life, giving women an opening to financial and legal independence: communities ceased to function as little fiefdoms, men and women alike moved in droves from feudal estates to the town centres (where after a year they were ostensibly free of their lord), town burgher and town council rule replaced the feudal system, and women persistently and as a matter of course used these new developments to take their place in the work force. As modifications in family life, in the business sphere, and in individual towns' political makeup both reflected and were themselves reflected in the larger societal overhaul, women seized the opportunity presented to them to participate as visible members of the world outside the home. In banking, merchant, and manufacturing centres such as Ghent, Bruges, Cologne, Lübeck, Strasbourg, Frankfurt on Main, Nuremberg, Regensburg, Zurich, and Basle, in royal residences such as London, Paris, Prague, and Vienna, and in less-populated trading and manufacturing towns, women assumed greater control over their own and their families' affairs, changing the face of town

life. 'Town air makes one free', the saying went. And with little, if any, resort to strikes or militant action, women claimed their share in the midst of sweeping social upheaval. *The Legend of Good Women* examines the living and working conditions of female town dwellers throughout the Middle Ages, when the great mass of those who would become what we shall call European town burghers shook themselves free of a thoroughly outmoded system of feudal rule.

In the days when business trips ate up weeks and weeks of travel time, when most goods were still produced painstakingly by hand, and when women were hamstrung by anachronistic legal restrictions and the whole society still groaned under the weight of feudal business practices, active participation by a woman in the viable and sometimes fabulously prosperous trade network that crisscrossed Europe required endless planning, enormous expenditures of effort, personal sacrifice, and often a simple sense of adventure. A significant number of businesswomen kept richly detailed records of their enterprises, and for help in reconstructing their work we have made liberal use of their autobiographical writings. Other material used includes town and court records, *Schöffensprüche* (collections of judicial sentences passed by lay judges), contracts, citizen registration lists, wills, and photographs. Among the more traditional sources tapped were certificates, tax registers, legal documents concerning town legislation, and town chronicles. In addition the work of Eileen Power, Régine Pernoud, Margret Wensky,

Shulamith Shahar, and Edith Ennen and the documents compiled by Peter Ketsch have proved indispensable. *Women and Daily Life in the Late Middle Ages (Frau im spätmittelalterlichen Alltag)*, published by the Austrian Academy of Sciences, provided a valuable model for research methods. The aim throughout has been to see female town dwellers as they actually were in their everyday lives.

The increasingly visible role of women in medieval town life found expression in the more progressive art and literature of the period, though ultimately, of course, the gains made by women were grossly incomplete and their elevation in status in some respects was later reversed. Legislation that granted women rights they had not had previously came slowly, if at all, with the stagnation explained partially by a well-established legal tradition that favoured the dominant role of men in marriage and partly, too, by the Catholic church's throwback stance on women. Women's relationship with the church was not simple. It ranged from emancipation attempts within the framework of the mendicant orders to the guarantee of material security to unmarried or widowed women in convents and Beguine foundations. While convents and town monasteries could be seen as a way out—the means to an education—entrance into these institutions could just as easily represent a forfeiture of personal freedom. As for marriage within church law, existing jurisdiction bound many women in ways they often preferred not to be tied.

In the pages that follow, we have tried to present as true a picture as possible of the relative improvement in the position of women that took place in the Middle Ages, the causes and conditions leading up to such change, and the obstacles faced by those who effected it.

Stadtluft macht frei (Town Air Makes One Free)? — The Female Town Dweller and the Emancipation of the Town Inhabitants from Feudal Rule

* From the twelfth century onward town citizens carried out their struggle for as much freedom as possible from the spiritual and secular rulers under the banner 'town air makes one free', a slogan that, however, was coined in the nineteenth century only. According to medieval town law, every citizen who had not been reclaimed by a feudal lord after a year and a day acquired personal freedom. In the pages that follow, we will look at the significance of this claim to women's lives. The change in women's circumstances in the medieval town can perhaps best be understood if we acquaint ourselves first with women's position in the work and home environment, in marriage and the family, during the early Middle Ages. Economic activity and social and legal position corresponded entirely to the requirements of the early feudal society, a society shaped to a large extent by both the dependent status of the direct producers and the rule of the feudal nobility. Because of the male right to inherit property and land, enshrined in tribal custom and common law of the sixth to the ninth centuries, a patriarchal mode of behaviour typified the way in which the two sexes coexisted. This was particularly true of marriage.

Marriage as the basic unit of social relations was initially recognized only for the nobility and for those free from feudal bondage. It existed in the form of *Raubehe* (robber marriage) or, with the collaboration of the bride, as elopement; *Friedelehe* or *Muntehe* were the other options (the first was marriage without a contract; the second involved a marriage contract and was more binding; both are explained below). It was in order to protect the interests of the feudal nobility, whose concerns were largely property and inheritance rights, that *Muntehe*—marriage on a strictly regulated contract basis—became the norm. Monogamy, backed by both the Church and the law, allowed the wives of the feudal nobility to be entrusted with the task of ruling, even when the men were away at war or carrying out official duties. Although this kind of absence frequently occurred, it did not lead to a breakdown of the patriarchal character of marriage, which was firmly established through the confluence of Germanic and Roman-Christian legal custom.

Tribal laws had excluded free women from any public office. Women were not permitted to appear independently in court but had to be represented by a man. He was the executor of a guardianship *(Munt)*, which incorporated the roles of protector, superior, and representative. The guardian *(Muntwalt)* was the father in the case of unmarried women and the husband in the case of married women. If the father or husband was dead, the closest male relative in the male line assumed guardianship. Apart from representing his charge in court, the guardian had the right to dispose of or use his ward's property; to mete out punishment, which in extreme cases could mean the death sentence; to give her away in marriage as he saw fit; and even to sell her.

Muntehe was widespread in western and central Europe and was practised through the drawing up of a marriage contract, in which the woman had no say whatsoever. It guaranteed the bridegroom his bride as well as guardianship over her and the former guardian, the father, a sort of transfer fee—a sum of money to be paid by the bridegroom in return for the transfer of guardianship from the girl's family to him. The marriage ceremony, a huge banquet to which all the relatives were invited, incorporated a legal-symbolic act to mark the transfer of guardianship. The bridegroom took his bride by the hand to indicate he now possessed her, or he could assert his right by kicking or kneeing her. He also acquired the rights to her property and her 'morning gift', a present—property, livestock, etc.—which he, according to law, had to give to his new wife after their first night as husband and wife. On her husband's death the woman became the ward of his family.

However, in the sixth century, Frankish law, which was to have a strong influence on the development of feudal relations in the northern part of central Europe, had already introduced limitations on the husband's right to his wife's property. It limited his right to her immobile property by permitting him merely to administer it—that is, he could not sell it. Since the dowry or marriage portion (the *Dos*) was, according to Frankish law, no longer handed over to the bride's parents or closest relatives but to the bride herself, the husband's rights over his wife's property were limited. This was significant because it meant that some financial provision was made for widows. Women could dispose of clothing and jewellery—the so-called *Gerade*—as they wished.

The legal status of the widow was unaffected by these changes. In the northern part of central Europe it was still determined by Saxon tribal law. This imposed great limitations on the personal freedom of the widow and placed her in the custody of the eldest son of the deceased husband's first marriage, the brother-in-law, or another close male relative on the husband's side. Lombard laws were more favourable to widows, and allowed them to remarry a free man of their own choice. They forbade the forcing of widows into convents before a period of one year had elapsed. Records and capitularies left by Prince Aregis from the end of the eighth century give the impression that the Lombard widows exploited their freedoms to the full: that having survived the first husband and thus got rid of his guardianship they were seized by a new zest for life:

> Thus some ladies after the death of their husbands, when they no longer have to submit to their husband's authority, are completely unrestrained in the use they make of their newfound freedom. Within the four walls of their own houses they may put on a nun's habit in order not to submit once more to a new husband. For they are secure in everything, so they think, provided they are not subjected to a new husband. And thus under the cover of religious life, they abandon all modesty and follow wherever their hearts lead them. They lead a life of pleasure, feasting, drinking, going to bathhouses and abuse their status by indulging in all sorts of clothes and luxuries. When they stroll down the streets they make up their faces and powder their hands in order to set the hearts of passers-by on fire.[1]

Although *Muntehe* was recognized as the approved form of marriage, *Friedelehe*, a sort of mini-marriage, was also tolerated. This did not involve the husband having custodianship over the wife but was a voluntary arrangement of the partners. It could be dissolved at any time in favour of *Muntehe*. The husband was not obliged to make a dowry for the bride. *Friedelehe* was particularly suited to the life-style of travelling merchants who spent long stretches of time away from home. For this reason it survived as a form of marriage in some towns (as did the practice of allowing the priest to have a concubine) right into the period of fully developed feudalism. In 1018, in *De diversitate temporum*, Alpert von Metz criticised the marital behaviour of the merchants of Tiel on the lower Rhine from the church's point of view: 'Unfaithfulness is no crime for them. As long as the woman holds her tongue, the man can do what evil he will, and nobody apart from the woman concerned may force him to account for his behaviour before the synod'.[2]

Barragania, a practice similar to *Friedelehe*, became common in Spain during the Reconquest. It was kept secret but was the accepted form of clerical marriage in Reconquest settlements.

Despite the threat of legal punishment within the practice of common law (introduced to Alamannic law circa 725, to Saxon and Thuringian law in 802/3), *Raubehe* remained another alternative form of cohabitation for the nobility and free men for many years to come.

The majority of the population, however, the feudal-dependent peasants, lived together in accordance with common-law procedures. These families were economically and legally dependent on the landowner and had to get his consent before a marriage could take place. Marriage between dependents of different landlords usually required that a substitute of the same sex be provided for the estate that was losing a body through the marriage. Agreements made between landlords in such cases also contain paragraphs on what services might be required from any children resulting from the marriage. In some areas the landowner retained throughout the Middle Ages the right to give his consent to marriage and on the death of a tenant the entitlement to some of the inheritance; this part was called the *mainmorte* in France and *Sterbefall* or *Besthaupt* in Germany.

In areas where socage farming—tenure of land of a lord in return for rendering agricultural and economic services—predominated, women were employed in the fields, woods, stables, or home, depending on the composition of the work force. Due to the extremely low level of both basic tools used in agriculture and land cultivation, any rise in output levels depended primarily on the physical input of the peasant population. On the other hand, repeated famines brought many deaths, and this meant that women of childbearing age had to be protected to a certain extent. For this reason a relatively stable division of labour between the sexes was established. Men as a rule tackled the plowing, mowing, threshing, grooming the draught animals, stubbing, and felling of trees. Women helped in the vineyards and with harvests. They also cultivated fibre plants, vegetables and herbs, gathered berries, managed the dairying and—to some extent—kept the cattle. They baked bread, made malt and beer, and produced candles, soap, earthenware vessels, and plant and animal dyes. The latter involved all stages of the process, from harvesting the plants (flax, hemp) and sheep shearing to producing clothing and other objects.

The demand of the secular and spiritual lords in early feudalism for textiles was also filled by workshops, called *gynaecea* (rooms for women to work and live in), which produced and dyed textiles and were run by women. The landlords supplied the raw materials and tools and in return gave the women accommodation, food, and clothing. The seven women who worked in the *gynaeceum* of the Werden estate on the Ruhr were allocated 104 bushels of rye per annum, 80 of barley, 148 of oats, 222 of other grain, 10 of beans, and probably a small amount of money. Around A.D. 800 the socage farm Staffelsee in the diocese of Augsburg employed 24 women in a cloth workshop. They produced, among other items, belted woollen garments and shirts. There were two *gynaecea* in the Ottonic palatinate of Tilleda. Judging by the weaving weights found during excavations there, they were also clothmakers. These sunken houses were situated alongside other farm buildings in the outskirts of the royal palatinate. Their size (one was 29 metres long and 6 metres wide, the other 15.5 metres long and 4.5 metres wide) suggests that they could have housed 22 to 24 women.

The workshops could in no way satisfy contemporary demand, which was not limited to the needs of the monks, nuns, serfs and maids. Often when ownership of a workshop was transferred to a monastery, it was still obliged to deliver a certain amount of textiles per year, such as linen shirts and woollen garments, to the previous owner. When the abbey of Reichenau took over a workshop in 816 it was obliged to deliver one woollen and two linen dresses per year, 6 foot and 2 hand garments, a piece of headwear, 1 bedcover, and 1 woollen blanket once every two years.

In order to cover the considerable demand for textile goods, the wives of the feudal serfs were also obliged to supply the landlords. Staffelsee's 19 yards had to supply the landlord with one shirt and one surplice per year. The bondsmen on the estate of the Reichenau abbey lived in Wickenhausen and were allowed to choose from about 844 onward whether they paid their dues in grain or in female textile work (textura feminae). The demand for particularly precious textiles for Catholic church services was also filled by nuns in the convents attended by the female aristocracy.

* From the eleventh century onward the level of agricultural productive resources in the developed areas of western and central Europe had permitted a sedentariness of and a visible increase in the population. The division of labour within agricultural and craft production had developed on a large scale, and a considerable number of non-agrarian urban centres sprang up. Not all of them were new topographical settlements. The civitates of Roman times also existed—though by name only—in the early Middle Ages, and there is evidence that some of them had never been abandoned, retaining cultural-religious or state-administrative functions, or sometimes a combination of both. In these early medieval towns some rudimentary craftwork was practised, but economic welfare was still based on the agricultural sector. Towns such as Vienna, Grenoble, Arles, Cologne, and Mainz used a substantial part of their walled land for crop-growing. Towns without such historical roots also began to appear: settlements that mushroomed in places that were strategic from the point of

view of transport, having river estuaries, river banks and firths, or river or road junctions. Usually the nobility, in connection with fortresses and other feudal centres, such as monasteries and bishops' residences, undertook planned urban expansion in order to promote the economic development of their estates or to guarantee military back-up for their political interests. All these medieval settlements, however they were founded, expanded during the eleventh and twelfth centuries to become medieval towns with a completely new economic structure characterised by independent small goods production and exchange of goods with other settlements. Because of their different roots, the first western and central European towns had a colourful mixture of citizens. In the flourishing towns there were tenant farmers and serfs as well as the estate officials of the local feudal town lords or of the land-owning cloisters, ecclesiastical foundations, or other religious institutions within the town walls and suburb areas, and there were increasing numbers of professional merchants who were protected by the king and numerous peasant farmers who either were landless or had run away from their landlord. The exchange of goods between manufacturing towns and agriculture expanded. There were more and more possibilities for manufacture and merchant enterprise.

A decisive prerequisite for this increased trade was provided by the new property relations, according to which the craftsman and merchant could operate independently of any feudal lord. More and more, both were free to organise and dispose of their labour as they wished. Interesting in this connection are the court regulations of the episcopal estate in the flourishing town of Worms, dating from 1023/25. These guarantee the widow, or in the case of her death the sons or nearest relatives of the husband, the right to the marriage portion 'and to everything she undisputedly possesses after one year and one day'. Laws governing marriage property or other inheritances had to be respected provided that the marriage partners had agreed to them before reliable witnesses. If, on the death of both parents, a son and daughter were left behind, the son inherited the land, which was liable to feudal service, and the daughter the clothes of the mother and 'anything else mobile and made by her'. Everything else had to be divided between son and daughter.

* The town inhabitants who already occupied a fairly strong position from both an economic and social point of view gained considerable strength from the beginning of the eleventh century through the commune movement. They set about removing any obstacles that could stop them from enjoying to the full the benefits of their new way of life. These obstacles included the rights of the feudal town lords to impose custom duties, control the markets, retain certain judicial rights, and charge levies for the building and upkeep of the town walls. The townsfolk also set about abolishing the privileges of religious institutions. The commune movement was an expression of the economic, political, and intellectual maturity of the medieval town citizen. Depending on local power relations, the citizens used various methods and means to guarantee themselves a secure place within feudal society. If they were cunning enough to exploit financial difficulties experienced by the feudal town lords, they could acquire important rights and privileges by making large cash payments to them. In Italy and France from the twelfth century onward, intellectual confrontation with the traditional thought of the Catholic church coincided with the growing economic strength of the towns. This came about partly because representatives of the town citizenry were joining socioreligious movements. The *coniurationes* were another expression of the town citizens' striving toward emancipation—of their attempts to achieve independent representation of their economic, social, and political interests. These associations included all citizens living within the town boundaries. They took an oath binding them to mutual protection—even, if necessary, against the town lords.

The achievement of full or almost full independence from the town lords in the most important west and central European urban economic centres in the course of the commune movement (or the establishing of important individual privileges through the town councils, which were just beginning to gain strength) rendered the saying *Stadtluft macht frei*, 'town air makes one free', true within the town walls. The legal affairs of the merchants and craftsmen—who, since the twelfth century had achieved a special legal position compared with the officials of the feudal town and clearly labelled themselves *burgenses*—were on the whole now in the hands of the town court. The burgher first gained definite legal status of his own in Italy and Flanders. Even around the year 1100 the northern Italian towns had their own administrative body, the *consules*. These became firmly established institutions in the twelfth century, when the number of towns with their own burgher administrative body grew—Laon in 1128, Reims late in the century, Basle and Speyer in 1190, Strasbourg after 1190, Utrecht in 1196, and Lübeck in 1201. The council consisted of members (*consules*) elected by the town citizens and it represented the political, social, and economic interests of the town community. It had an extremely positive influence on the further development of trade and simple goods production.

Kings, princes, and other feudal powers saw their chance to increase their financial income with the growing economic power of the towns and the extension of goods–money relations. From the middle of the twelfth century until about 1300, a series of towns were founded in central Europe. Some of them were granted very favourable privileges by the feudal town lords. The only towns that survived, however, were those with the energy of the economically active burghers behind them. The burghers even had a say in the wording of the town's legal charter. Because the towns often looked for an existing model, whole legal districts or 'families' were formed whose 'mothers' were, for example, Magdeburg, Lübeck, Frankfurt on Main, Nuremberg,

Vienna, Aachen, Freiburg im Breisgau, Brunswick, Dortmund, and Soest in Germany. The feudal powers of central and western Europe helped to boast the economic position of markets and market places by granting them privileges. Thus a range of town life was established in Italy, France, Bohemia, Poland, Germany, England, and Spain that lasted until the fourteenth century. Because of its variety—it encompassed towns whose wealth was created through the export of manufactured goods, long-distance trading, mining, medium-scale trade, and manufacturing as well as agrarian settlements with some urban features—this set of towns provided European feudal society with an economic dynamism of its own. The formation of autonomous councils with full administrative and extensive legal authority discouraged the nobility from demanding the return of peasant farmers who had fled to the town, since they were on the whole guaranteed personal freedom after a period of one year and one day had passed. They in turn provided the population reservoir necessary for the growth of the town economy.

✳ What does the struggle for the free development of trade and crafts—for the political and intellectual freedom of the town citizenry on the one hand and the granting of favourable privileges by the feudal town lords on the other—have to do with the lives of the female population in medieval towns?

The town offered, as mentioned above, various possibilities for both the merchant or the craftsman to make a profit. The idea was to accumulate at least some financial capital, no matter how small. This meant keeping family property together and leading a fairly frugal existence. This in turn placed certain demands on the women, since they were responsible for clothing the family and for spinning, weaving, sewing, and knitting. In order to ensure that the family fortunes did not go downhill, those women whose husbands were travelling merchants had to take care of business and show around business partners who arrived unannounced; make payments; collect information about the state of affairs in the local market; and seek out prospective partners for their sons and daughters. Women were also used within the independent family businesses for tasks traditionally performed by them—for example, producing textiles, rope making, malt, beer, and bread making, and working in hostelries and inns. Thus an extremely narrowly defined interest group was formed within the urban economic setup comprising parents and unmarried children. It was undoubtedly very important for craftsman and merchant families to hang onto the property they had managed to amass, including their workshops and tools, in order to hand it down to their heirs. The women therefore took on another important role: that of protecting the inheritance not only from the claims of the feudal lords but from the customary claims of relatives.

The town lords often tried to interfere with the interests of the town inhabitants: they demanded part of the inheritance; seduced women, daughters, and wards of the citizens; married the daughters and widows of burghers to their own people in order to have a claim to their family fortune and demanded particularly high payments when free people married one of the serfs or when descendants of serfs married into another town or estate. These policies of the feudal lords toward traders and craftsmen affected family interests and directly touched the lives of women. They were part of the long, drawn-out battle between town lords and the burghers, which exploded during the commune movement.

At first glance it seems astonishing that the written sources documenting the conflict between the *coniurationes* and the feudal town lords hardly mention the participation of women. An exception in the written documentation is the report by Guibert of Nogent about the events in Amiens in 1115 connected with the commune movement. Guibert writes in his *vita* of women's involvement in the four-year-long struggle between the citizens in the *coniurationes* and their town lords (the count and his castellan). The military victory of the citizens depended on seizing a tall and sturdy tower occupied by the town lords. The stronghold had to be attacked by overwhelming them with a pelter of stones launched from towers especially built for the occasion. Apparently eighty women took part in the stone pelting. Women also appeared to have been active in the conflicts of 1111 in Laon. More often, however, it is to be assumed that women are among the faceless crowds who for example in Magdeburg were mobilised through religious arguments to fight for the goals of the *coniurationes*.

Despite the apparently minimal participation of women in the commune movement, the results of that movement were of vital importance for the further transformation of their living conditions. Legal concessions made by the feudal town lords (in the form of town charters) as a result of the demands made by citizens in the commune movement or of preemptory concessions by the town lords paved the way for changes in the life of the female citizen. The principle of granting the female burgher the privileged status of town inhabitant was a fundamental prerequisite for all further progressive developments in the economic, social, and legal conditions of the women in the towns. In the legal statutes of, for example, those towns founded in Spain during the Reconquest, or Bremen in 1186, or Stade in 1209, the basic right of citizens to be free provided they have been within the legal town boundaries for one year and one day is expressly guaranteed for both men and women. This clear extension of town freedom to cover women had actually been preceded in some towns by individual concessions with regard to women's legal status.

One of the earliest privileges was granted in Halberstadt. In order to encourage trade in his diocese Bishop Burchard II granted in the second half of the eleventh century the right of succession to his merchants' daughters. Even more far-reaching rights were granted by the kings of Navarre from the second half of the eleventh century onward within the framework of settlement freedoms. They extended the right of succession to the daughters of all the inhabitants. The privilege in question granted by King Sancho in 1212 stems from an older one bestowed in the suburb St. Saturnin of Pamplona which in turn goes back to a privilege of 1063 *(Fuero de Jaca)*: 'I have granted and bestowed this favour, as is written above, upon you and your sons and daughters and all your heirs, so that you may possess everything safely and securely and freely for ever after'.[3] As in this case, the new towns founded in Belgium (Geraardsbergen/Grammont) and in the southwest of Germany also established the principle of equality of man and woman, son and daughter in the right to succession in order to attract settlers.

In bestowing market rights in Freiburg im Breisgau in the twelfth century, Duke Conrad of Zähringen proclaimed that 'to all future and present citizens, I, Conrad, have established a market in this town of Freiburg. . . . I have decreed, in a sworn agreement with the honourable merchants summoned from all over, that they should begin and expand the market area'. Under the individually listed rights a prominent position is given to the following guarantee: 'If one of my burghers dies, his wife and children should inherit everything: everything her husband leaves behind belongs to them and cannot be sequestered by others'.[4]

Limitations on the town inhabitants' right to inherit were also abolished step by step in Worms and Speyer. Favours granted by Henry V to Speyer in 1111 and Worms in 1114, reaffirmed and extended by Frederick I (Barbarossa) in 1182 and 1184, liberated all inhabitants from paying inheritance tax. In these older towns, which had a very different population structure in fact and in law, the granting of the right of inheritance to all citizens signalled an end to the old, deep-rooted feudal laws and heralded a step forward in the consolidation of various groups of townspeople into a unified town community. In Worms, for example, there were the Friesian merchants who were responsible for the Rhine trade, the vassals of the estate belonging to the Alsatian abbey Murbach, and the most numerous group, the *urbani*, townsfolk.

The privileges bestowed by town lords upon male and female inhabitants represent, however, anything but a break with the family inheritance laws. They refer only to the abolishment of the former right of feudal lords to some of the inheritance. When Conrad of Zähringen stated that the wife and children of a burgher should keep the inheritance and that no one else could stake a claim to it, he referred only to the claims made formerly by the feudal lords. The contemporary family inheritance law put the married woman under the custodianship of her husband. He had the guardianship over the family property and also, as a rule, represented his wife in court. The widow, according to the town inheritance laws, was at a disadvantage due to the priority given to children in inheritance law. On remarriage, the widow was frequently entitled only to a child's share of the inheritance. The priority given by the town legislation to securing any family fortune for the successors is seen clearly in the town law of Fribourg in Uechtland. Here the widow was only granted *Niessbrauchrecht*, the right to use the inheritance, and was considered merely the temporary administrator of her children's property. On remarriage she lost even this function. A change in favour of women only came about at the end of the twelfth century, when, due to the changing economic situation and the increasing need for women's independent help in trade and craftwork, the right of both marriage partners to the property they created together (the right stems from Frankish law) began to be recognized. The renunciation of the claims of feudal lords to a share of the inheritance was an important prerequisite for the unfettered development of family property and inheritance law along lines that favoured the interests of the town burghers.

Likewise, the abolition of the necessity of obtaining the approval of a feudal lord before getting married was of vital importance for the formation of the town burghers as a new social force, and for the raising of the so-cial position of the female town dweller in the early phase of the urban emancipation movement. In Speyer and Worms the continuing practice of marriage limitations and the related practice of allowing commissioners of the town lords to dissolve marriages between inhabitants of different social groups, or to put certain groups at a disadvantage through property laws, aroused great dissent among those directly affected and indeed among all of the town population. The favours granted by Henry V and their reaffirmation by Frederick I (Barbarossa) abolished these disadvantages in inheritance law for marriages between partners with a different personal legal status and guaranteed the inhabitants of these towns the freedom to choose their own partners.[5]

The right of citizens to choose marriage partners for their children was included in the Speyer town law, which Frederick II granted to the town of Anweiler in 1219. In 1264 the inhabitants of Winterthur were granted the same right, and the municipal charter passed by King Magnus Harkonarson for Bergen in Norway included a similar clause. Another version of marriage freedom for women was the abolition of the regulation forcing daughters and widows of burghers to marry members of the royal socage farm or officials of the royal court. This was abolished in 1232 for the German towns of Frankfurt on Main, Wetzlar, Friedberg, and Gelnhausen. In 1199 Eleanor, or Aliénor, queen consort of Henry II of England and duchess of Aquitaine, confirmed the privileges of the citizens of Poitiers they had been granted by her predecessors. She referred to the right freely to choose marriage partners for their daughters. This right was likewise granted to every free woman. In the same year, Eleanor granted the inhabitants of the Saintonge the abolition of regulations forcing daughters and widows of burghers to marry certain persons. These privileges included the free disposal of the inheritance of the burghers. In 1128 the French town of Laon and in 1212 the Austrian town of Enns were granted charters which confirmed the equal legal status of men and women as compared with the feudal town lord.

Freedom to choose one's own marriage partner did not of course mean that there was complete freedom to follow one's own inclination *(Neigungsehe)* in choosing a partner. Children of burghers had their marriages arranged by their parents or closest relatives and guardians in accordance with the economic and political interests of the family. The abolition of the need to get the consent of the feudal lord for marriage was, however, important, because the burghers could then arrange marriages that served to further promote its economic and political power. In choosing, the burghers gave top priority not to the extent of the potential partner's fortune but rather to the political role played by the family being married into—the connections to be gained through relatives of the family, its social status, and its access to town offices.

It was absolutely necessary for the prospective bride to have an untarnished reputation. Hence the importance of another aspect of town freedom: the guarantee of greater personal protection through the law. This concerned primarily protection against abduction, rape, and slander. In the Austrian, Polish and German town laws of the thirteenth century the desire of the town burghers to be guaranteed protection is evident. Punishment for abduction and rape could be the death sentence or outlaw. This was permitted, for example, by the town laws of Haimburg, Wiener Neustadt, Neumarkt, Zwickau, and Halle. Despite what would now be considered dubious procedure—the presentation of evidence—threat of such severe punishment seems to have had effect. In order to prove that she had been raped, the woman had to bring forward witnesses, usually two, at least one of them a man.

In extreme cases a town (such was the case with Halle on the Saale) could require seven so-called scream witnesses. The chronicle kept by Matthias von Neuenburg tells us that the burghers were prepared to take political action if their women's legal right to personal protection was abused. Referring to the town lord of Neuenburg, a town in Breisgau, he writes in 1218: 'This Heinrich came to Neuenburg with the intention of receiving oaths of allegiance from his people. In the evening he brought dishonour upon the wife of a burgher, and as a result the people of Neuenburg refused to make their oaths before him'.[6]

With notable solidarity, the burghers of this economically insignificant town on the Rhine made it clear through their lack of subservience to the town lord, a son of the Count of Freiburg, that respect for town freedom of both man and woman, whether written or unwritten, was for them the most important law.

Thus in these towns a new line of legal thought, favourable to the development of the female personality, began to be accepted in the second half of the eleventh century and to find even stronger expression in the twelfth century. The associations in which women—not only wives—were equal members, played a prominent role in this process, which fitted in with the socio-family interests of the medieval town burghers and which could not be suppressed by the dogmatic doctrine of the Catholic church.

The change in the living conditions of the female town dweller now depended to a large extent on whether she herself could fulfill the expectations placed upon her; whether she could tackle the new tasks ahead of her. These tasks included first and foremost sharing some of the business and other commitments, the economic interests of her husband, assuming joint responsibility for securing the family inheritance, and providing the children with a higher level of education in order to meet the requirements of merchant life and simple goods production.

Women as Merchants and Traders

✳ The top urban economic centres in western and central Europe from the twelfth and thirteenth centuries onward were those towns which, due to their geographical position, had acquired an important role in sea and transit trade: Venice, Genoa, Pisa, Marseilles, Paris, Bruges, London, Cologne, and Lübeck. Also important were the towns that produced and traded in important raw materials or were centres for simple goods production and had acquired, through specialisation, a reputation for quality. The latter type included textile centres in northern Italy, Flanders/northern France, the Rhine area, and northern Germany and metal production and processing centres such as Liège, Cologne, and the brass-producing centres on the Maas.

The growing number of trading cooperatives shows how eager numerous French, English, and German towns were to find and extend export outlets for their own production. As the owners of raw materials, tools, and products, the craftworkers were concerned with regulating the acquisition of raw materials, training the apprentices, and controlling production and sales. As a result of these efforts by simple goods producers and the opening up of more domestic and overseas markets, the late thirteenth century saw a marked specialisation in the crafts. It saw, too, a rapid increase in specialisation by towns and regions in the production and refinement of certain products. Thus the town of Constance exported linen from the whole of the Lake Constance area. Augsburg, Isny, Kempten, St. Gallen, and Ulm exported linen produced in the surrounding area. In woollen cloth weaving, the quality of production was set on the international market by textile centres in Flanders and northern France—Arras, Douai, Tournai, Provins, and Rouen, and competition was provided by the Italian and, since the mid-fourteenth century at the latest, by English production. German production expanded because of the mass demand for cheap cloth on the local market. The technical wherewithal for large-scale production of textile goods had been introduced with the pedal-operated loom, the hand-spinning wheel, and the use of water mills for fulling cloth.

With the application of investment-intensive equipment such as fulling mills and the greater need to monitor the work process and its end products (due to the quality required for export and the need to remain competitive), guild organisations began to take root in many places. Simultaneously, however, the town councils in trading towns that were interested in expanding export tried to increase their control over the guilds.

In spite of the drastic effect of periodic outbreaks of disease, especially the plague, the crafts experienced another distinct boom in the second half of the fourteenth century. The factors contributing to this upswing were: the closer links between the newly formed textile centres in Flanders and England with the traditional large trading centres; the specific gearing of an individual craft toward export; the rapid diffusion of the most advanced technology; a growing knowledge of chemical processes; and the mobilisation of additional manpower, including female labour.

In the fourteenth and fifteenth centuries the mining and crafting of precious metals experienced a huge boom in almost all European countries. With the development of the metalworking crafts, it was possible to produce better tools, to make simple machines, and to improve weapon technology. The technical changes in mining and metal processing had an effect on a whole number of other trades—shipbuilding, construction, loading, and transport. New trades such as paper production, book printing, and glass production developed. Individual towns specialised in the production and refining of certain products.

The development of trade and simple goods production brought about dramatic changes in feudal society which would have been impossible without the deployment of all the economic forces within the town burghers, including the forces within the family. The backup provided by women for the diverse economic and professional activities of their husbands, brothers, and sons proved invaluable. The legal status of the medieval town burghers, which to a large extent accounted for their economic, social, and political position, allowed them to do more than merely form an 'estate' within the feudal system. Rather they achieved a propertied status which had a dramatic effect on their work and home lives. Openings were created for women in craftwork, in large- and small-scale trading, in banking and money lending, in hostelries and inns, and in numerous other trades.

The successful participation in the accumulation of the family wealth and in the expansion of the family's economic and social influence made it more practical and feasible for women to have an independent professional life. Women were successful in quite a broad spectrum of professions which often demanded a high level of intellectual ability. This process was encouraged by the fact that members of the upper strata in the towns and sometimes even the town councils showed an increasing interest in the upbringing and education of young girls and women from the prosperous burghers.

✳ The female town dweller was initially most active, and contributed to the greatest extent and most consistently to economic prosperity, in trade and finance. The source materials through which one can trace female activity in the trading sector go back to a very early date. The earliest examples are recorded in the registers of the public notaries in Venice, Genoa, and Marseilles. The Italian notary registers suggest that there were independent female merchants even at the beginning of the thirteenth century. They appear a little later in the corresponding French sources.

The Italian maritime towns, as well as being market and sea-trading centres of international importance, were also the birthplace of modern (medieval) banking and trading practices. The letter of credit and the trading company, for example, were, from a very early date, an integral part of trading activity with the Arab countries and with northern Europe.

In these Italian maritime towns, which were open to all the new demands made on them by the medieval town middle classes, the wealthy female burgher could, even in the early thirteenth century, participate actively in long-distance trading without herself ever having to undergo the rigours of a lengthy voyage. She could invest her financial capital in trading companies and thus enable less wealthy but enterprising partners to participate in the economic expansion of the Mediterranean area. As the investor or the supplier of goods, these merchant women shared both profit and loss. One of the oldest surviving contracts records the involvement of a female burgher from Genoa in such a trading company.

In 1201 the widow of Rubaldus de Antimonus entrusted her trading partner with linen to the value of ten Genoese pounds for sale in Ceuta, Morocco. The company was a so-called *commande*: a shipowner or a trader embarking on an overseas voyage would take charge of goods bought by a partner with capital, in return for a 25-percent share of the profit. This was not a unique occurrence. In 1206 another female burgher from Genoa, Mabilia, the mother of Otto Lecavela, signed a trade

1 Mary, portrayed as the queen of heaven on her throne, receives
the Three Kings, against the charming background of a stylised
medieval town.
Panel painting by Guido da Siena, 'Adoration of the Magi',
ca. 1270. Staatliches Lindenau Museum, Altenburg

Following pages

2 Women look after the children and family possessions during the
great fire of Berne in 1286.
Miniature from Diebold Schilling, *Spiezer Bilder-Chronik*, 1485,
plate 35. Municipal and University Library, Berne

3 Noble governors rob women and maidens, while to the right in
the background the husbands and fathers look on helplessly.
Abuse of marriage law and personal freedom left its mark in the
consciousness of the people.
Miniature from Diebold Schilling, *Spiezer Bilder-Chronik*, 1485,
plate 60. Municipal and University Library, Berne

Von einer großen brunst so
leider zu Bern geschach

So man zalt von der geburt unsers herren
und behalters Ihu cristi m cc lxxxxv iare
In der oster wuchen do verbran die Statt von
Bern von der tentz gassen uff untz an die alten
vinguine und wart darnach wider gebuwen

Vos alten langen ziten / c / das boen gestift
wart / hatten gros kriegy die dryg waltz
ltette / vre droitz vnd vunderwalden / das
ersten mit den herren von kburg / darnach mit
den herren von habspurg / vnd am letsten mit der
herrschaft von osturich.   Vnd vz der kriegen
voffnung / als die von droitz vnd vunderwaldsn

4 A trader conversing with a customer. She displays her wares: gloves and purses.
Painting by an artist from Upper Austria, 'Birth of the Virgin', ca. 1475/85, detail. The Parish Church of Kirchdorf-on-the-Krems

5 A female shopkeeper displays bags and spices in a shop that opens onto the street.
Miniature from the Codex of Baltazar Behem, 1505, plate 3. University Library, Cracow

6 A female shopkeeper with weighing scales. In front of the shop one sees the king in conversation with a merchant and his wife. Miniature from Schondoch, *Die Geschichte der Könige von Frankreich*, 1420 version. *Codex Vindobonensis 2675*, fol. 6 v. Österreichische Nationalbibliothek, Vienna

7 Well-versed in money matters, the wife takes over the task of bookkeeping.
Painting by Quentin Massys the Elder, 'The Banker and His Wife', 1520 (?). Staatliche Museen zu Berlin, Picture Gallery

Following pages

8 Pie makers in Constance bring their pastries filled with fine spices, meat or fish to a female assistant, who sells them. From Ulrich Richental, *Das Konzil zu Konstanz,* after a copy of 1465, fol. 23 v. Rosgartenmuseum, Constance

9 Women selling spices and herbs have joined fishmongers and snail sellers. From Ulrich Richental, *Das Konzil zu Konstanz,* after a copy of 1465, fol. 25 v. Rosgartenmuseum, Constance

1414

Die selb vorgenant botschaft macht ock die ordnung vmb alleg
ding vnd vmb anders wie man das halten vnd geben solt
die ward ock gehalten also lang das die ordnung vfzerstal
in die gegin allenthalb wie man yeglich ding geben solt vnd das man
allerlay dings so vil bracht das man es vil nacher gab kann die
ordnung gesetzt ward vnd des ersten was das korn allweg ein ge
namen koff do der korn allerding was do gab man ain mit keren
des aller besten vmb vviij schilling pfennig vnd gutten gemainen
koren esten mit vmb vij ß ß oder vmb vij ß ß das selb weri
nit lenger dann drej spital so es aller turost was darnach ward
geben amen mit keren des aller besten vmb vvj ß ß vnd darnach
vmb viij ß ß vnd es vij ß ß so pllichem koff do stund es gewonlich
das corrodium gantz vff das das kurn nit turer ward vnd fand man
sy allweg gnug das kain gebrest me dar an was daruch was oder ain
halb vff brot vmb ain pfennig oder viij vmb ain schilling das fand
man ock wie vil man wolt wann man bracht so vil vff wagen
vnd mit karren vnd ock zu schiffen das zu karren oder vil
fromder brotbeken zu costentz die stattglich vff dem markt bauchen
vnd der von costentz brotbeken ock ock waren brotbeken
zu Costentz die hetten ringe vnd klaine offenlin die furten sy vff
zwo redlin durch die stat vnd buchent die in bekeren vnd
fruig vnd kraestgellen vnd pllich brottes dero wurend etlich gefullt
mit klunen etlich mit voglin gevwuez mit gutter spezerey vnd
etlich mit flaysch vnd etlich mit vischen gebachen wie die amer
gern wolt haben dero fand man gnug In gelichem vnd gutten
koff vnd darnach sy kostlich waren vnd amer kosten wolt vnd
ist dis die figure

Fremde Brodbacker zu Constanz.

10 This view of Zurich shows, front left, the
guild house of the carpenters and, next to
it, the 'Wettingen houses'. The bridge leads
to the town hall, the river tower served as
a prison.
Panel painting by Hans Leu the Elder,
'Leusch Town View', 1492/96, detail.
Schweizerisches Landesmuseum, Zurich

Following page

11 Metal ledger showing Johan Lombard
(d. 1487), silk trader and councillor of
London, and his wife Anne (d. 1489) and her
six children in Hinseworth, Herefordshire.
In: Ruth and Michael Tennenhaus, *The
Immortal Image.* Leipzig, 1977.

contract with Rubaldus Galetta, probably with her son acting as mediator. Galetta took charge of Swabian linen and other linen cloth worth 88 pounds and 7 shillings for sale in Sicily in return for a 25-percent share in the profit.

An examination of the records of the Genoese public notaries in the first half of the thirteenth century reveals hundreds of such *commandes*: they account for about 8 percent of all the documents. Of those involved in such trade contracts, 21.1 percent were women. They provided 14.4 percent of the capital invested in seafaring ventures.[7]

Company contracts are also in evidence in Marseilles in the mid-thirteenth century. A balance sheet belonging to a certain Béatrix Raoline of Marseilles, who, as the daughter of a cloth trader was also in the business herself, tells us that in a deal with another cloth trader, Guillaume Lafont, she gave him 150 pounds as her stake in the company. Another woman from Marseilles, Cécile Roux, had a stake—goods worth 25 sous—in a shipload of goods bound for Saint-Jean-d'Acre, where the Marseilles long-distance traders had a branch. In this case the seller was entitled to a 50-percent share of the profit.

There is evidence of women's involvement in trading companies belonging to relatives from Genoese notary registers as early as 1205. Venice also provides examples. For the Rialto, accounts show the investments made by female citizens in such joint ventures dating from 1203, 1205, and 1231. Whereas these were trade agreements made between brothers and sisters, a different agreement dating from 1223 was made by a married woman with the relatives of her husband. The investment had been made in 1220, and repayment plus profit amounted to 75 Venetian pounds. Another woman from the Rialto was presented with several letters of credit in receipt of money previously invested in trading companies. The letter of credit written for her in 1233 concerns three trading credits worth more than 100 Genoese pounds which had been given in 1211 and 1212 to various people and which now had to be settled with Auticara, wife of Vendramo de Caluvrio.

Female members of families involved in long-distance trading based in the Italian maritime towns were clearly quite active in trade and money deals while their merchant husbands or male relatives were away on trips or were ill. Thus in 1206, Juleta, the wife of the Genoese trader Bonus Vasallus Crispini, who was away on a business trip, signed a company contract with Obertus Lungus. The latter was to deliver Swabian textile products worth 317 Genoese pounds to her husband in Ceuta. Should her husband not be found there, Obertus Lungus was entrusted with the task of selling the goods himself in return for a share in the profit. A Venetian lady by the name of Friutera seems to have had almost free access to her husband's wealth; in 1208 at Rialto she received payment of a trading credit which a certain Stefano Venier had been given by her husband.

Nor was it beneath the dignity of the wives of the Venetian doges to be involved in overseas trade. In 1209 Maria Ziani handed over a loan of 120 Venetian pounds to Tommaso Viadro for sea trading, for which the doge and his council gave their express approval. In this aspect the loan differed from other sea-trading loans made by women independently, where the husband's authorisation was not necessary. The fact that the wife of the most important state official in the Venetian City Republic gave loans to overseas traders with the express approval of her husband shows how close a link there was between this initial stage of active female involvement in overseas trade and the economic-political ambitions of the upper strata in the town.

The economic expansion of the Venetian maritime republic—seen clearly in the claims to the throne when the Latin Empire was founded in 1204—was based on the deployment of all the economic and social potential of the town. It is not therefore by chance that Constantinople, Alexandria, and Ceuta were among the destinations listed in the company trade contracts drawn up by Italian women.

The close connection between female merchant activity and the power struggles among the Mediterranean town burghers brought on by the crusades is mirrored in a company contract made between two female merchants in Marseilles on 6 July 1248. In the contract Marie Valence and Bernard Ambulet agree to set up a butcher's business on the islands situated just off the town (the Îles de Marseilles). Here the owners of large ships could be supplied with meat and other provisions before setting out to sea. Sailors and pilgrims could also make last-minute purchases before a long sea trip. The contract was drawn up at the time of the Seventh Crusade (1248–1254), which the French king Louis IX took part in. Business must have looked promising.

The Marseilles town council tried to bring supplies to all the ships in the harbour under its control by introducing new town laws. The town statutes of the thirteenth century strictly forbade the purchase of foodstuffs by ship's chandlers (*cargatores*) from harbour officials or their wives or children. The Marseilles city councillors (*consules*) also tried to control the activities of the grain merchants and their wives through legislation. The grain trade was a particularly important aspect of this maritime port since there was little agriculture in the surrounding area and its harbour was an important international shipping route. The town councillors demanded that the merchants who were involved in the grain trade in the service of the town should swear an oath that they would carry out the trade loyally and without deception. This oath was specifically required of the wives of the town grain merchants as well.

The period with which we are now concerned allows us to make a small excursion, for comparative purposes, outside of Europe into the Christian–Islamic area on the eastern shore of the Black Sea. Here Georgia was experiencing an economic and cultural boom under the reign of Queen Tamara (1184–1213), and it was here, at the beginning of the thirteenth century, that the Georgian poet Rust'aveli wrote *The Man in the Panther's Skin*. In his poem Rust'aveli gives detailed descriptions of the family and social duties of the wife of a president of a merchants' guild in a maritime town which was also a royal residence. In her husband's absence she receives and entertains visiting merchants, sees that the merchants' goods, which the merchants themselves had first to present to the guild president, are stored properly in caravanserais, or warehouses. She had, moreover, a representative function within the social circle of the local merchants' wives. With unconcealed pride she claims that 'just as my husband leads the guild merchants and is their spokesman, so do I lead the colourful guild of their wives to the queen's palace'. The official ceremony in the palace is followed by hospitality and entertainment in the house and garden of the guild president. 'Then towards evening I lead my guests into the garden; I entertain them there and show myself to be a good hostess. I call in the singers, because it cannot be that there is no singing on a festive day. Then I dance to the sound of the flute and violin, changing veils and headdress as the mood of the music requires'.[8]

Clearly those features of daily life shared by the maritime towns on the Mediterranean and the Black Sea were in no way limited to the continuing practice of keeping domestic slaves, which was actually of secondary importance for economic development. The similarities in the work and living conditions of the overseas traders are striking. As in the Italian maritime towns, the overseas traders did not yet have a highly organised system of trade representatives abroad, and therefore when they were away on their frequent business trips they had to entrust their wives with representing the business at home.

Female involvement in wholesale trading also took place north of the Alps, in towns that were engaged in trade and the export of manufactured goods. In Douai, the cloth-producing town in Flanders, women are mentioned as wool traders as early as the mid-thirteenth century. They were active as both merchants and cloth producers. The 1274 Hundred Rolls register in London lists those widows who were engaged in wholesale trade for wool and other products. In Lübeck the merchant women are referred to in the Latin town laws dating from the thirteenth century.

❋ In the fourteenth and fifteenth centuries female participation in trading companies had spread to other German towns. Such a company contract is for example mentioned in 1353 in the will of a Lübeck shopkeeper, Mechthild von Bremen. From a company called the Socia Lubbe, which she formed with another woman, she was owed 30 marks. Druitgen Kollers, from Cologne, also formed a company with just one other partner, for whom she marketed cloth in southern Germany. In the period between 1435 and 1505 another four ladies from Cologne were involved in trading companies with no more than two partners. The accounts of Runtinger's store in Regensburg also provide evidence of small to average investments made by women. In the period 1380–1530, 267 men and 39 women were involved in the Great Ravensburg Trading Company.

In Thuringia, Erfurt was the trading centre for woad, the blue dye that was in great demand throughout late sixteenth-century Europe before the arrival of indigo. Toward the end of the fifteenth century Katherina Amlingyn and her daughter ran a woad trading company in Erfurt with other partners, who are not mentioned by name, selling their product to southern and southeastern Europe via their representative in Görlitz. Around the eighth year of operation, twenty wagon-loads of woad exported to Görlitz and further afield to eastern and southeastern Europe were the subject of a legal suit brought before the Magdeburg lay assessors, whose legal judgements provided Görlitz town council with information about the trading activities of the company.

Although participation by women in new forms of medieval trading activity illustrates how the possibilities for female citizens to be professionally active in the medieval communes had increased, one should not forget that this was not typical for European town life as a whole. The independent female long-distance and

wholesale trader was as a rule a phenomenon to be found only in the most important overseas trade and export centres. But it would be safe to assume that they served as some sort of inspiration to their female contemporaries.

Let us remain for the moment with the female merchant (the mercatrix) treated in the sources—as the name suggests—as an appendage of the male merchant, or mercator. There is good source material describing the state of affairs in Cologne, which played an important role among the centres of German international trade and export. Here, for example, out of seventeen importers active in the period 1460–1468 one single woman was responsible for 24 percent of all the sugar imports. A significant proportion of the wine trade was also monopolised by women and this was apparently the case in Jena, Neuss, and Schwäbisch Hall. In the years 1468–1469 the female wine merchants of Cologne controlled 10 percent of the market. In the 1470s the proportion controlled by them was even greater. The women of Cologne also controlled a large proportion of the market in steel imports. Karyssa under Helmslegern, who was active in the sheet iron trade between 1452 and 1459, was responsible for 5.8 percent of the total exports, the equivalent of 103 containers. She also had a stake in copper imports; with a turnover of 624 hundredweight she controlled 1.4 percent of the market. In the period 1460–1469 another female metal goods merchant in Cologne imported 3,288 hundredweight of lead, which amounted to 9.4 percent of the market. Although relatively few Cologne ladies seem to have been active in the cloth trade (in 1419, 1421, 1423, and 1428 they were never fewer than two but never more than seven) their share of the market in the same years amounted to more than 30 percent. These impressive achievements of the Cologne female merchants could be supplemented by numerous other examples, particularly in the spice, drug, dye, cotton, and raw silk trades. And in the fourteenth and fifteenth centuries we come across women exporting raw materials and finished textile goods from the towns of London, Danzig, and Görlitz.

An Englishwoman called Rose of Burford was a wholesale wool merchant in London at the end of the fifteenth century. She was a member of the association of 'merchants of the staple' (merchants who had been granted the privilege of trading in a staple commodity, usually wool) and exported English wool to Calais. She was also married to a rich merchant and officer of the crown who had lent King Edward II a considerable sum of money for his war with Scotland. Even while her husband was alive she appears in the treasury's expenditure accounts, and after his death there is even more frequent mention of her activities in the wool trade. She put in at least five requests to the English royal court for the repayment of the loan given to the king by her husband. Finally she put forward the proposal that the sum due to her, which was to be repaid from income made through annual custom duty payments made to the king for wool and skins, be subtracted from her own tax payments as a wool exporter. (Once she had actually presented her case to the court and produced evidence of the royal debt, her proposal was accepted.)

Barbara, wife of Simon Eberlein of Görlitz, was a German wholesale wool merchant who in 1470 turned to the lay assessors of the town to demand payment due for a delivery of wool worth 120 marks. The debtor was unable to pay, and she applied to his guarantors. According to medieval law, whoever vouched for the credit-worthiness and readiness to pay of another had to honour the debt should the debtor himself not pay it. The Magdeburg lay assessors, to whom this woman merchant turned for advice, gave legal backing to her actions.

Another woman who was active in Görlitz as a wholesale merchant in the textile trade was called Agnes Fingerin; she was the daughter of one rich Görlitz clothmaker. As a merchant she made a considerable fortune for herself (her husband died in 1465 and she survived him by about fifty years). The year of her husband's death, when she was tying up her business before she set out on a journey to Rome, she sold goods to her brother-in-law for 500 Hungarian forinths and gave him her house, retaining for her own business activities during her lifetime the workroom (*Werggadem*) and the vaults. Apart from the goods worth 500 forinths, Agnes Fingerin possessed another 300 Hungarian forinths in 1475. These she paid in order to be exempted from any further municipal tax payments during her lifetime. By paying another $187^1/_2$ marks to the town council she was guaranteed an annual interest which was to be put at the disposal of the town hospitals. Even before this, in 1471, she had already established a fund for the poor of the town, which until quite recently still provided for the distribution of bread that was known as the *Agnetenbrot*.

A letter from Danzig addressed to the English town of Lynn is revealing with regard to the personal commitment of one Danzig lady to her trade; the letter, which dates from 1455, indicates that on several occasions this merchant was prepared to go personally to England in order to settle some trading deal.

* All over Europe, in Venice, Genoa, Marseilles, Strasbourg, Regensburg, Nuremberg, Cologne, Wiener Neustadt, Basle, Frankfurt on Main, Görlitz, Bamberg, and Völkermarkt on the Drava, the patrician upper strata in the towns indulged in trading partnerships between man and wife. Such partnerships undoubtedly depended not only on family interests and the level of education of the wife but also on her age. In her first marriage a young girl was usually too young and too inexperienced to be a business partner. In certain cases the young wife was, however, called upon to represent the family interests in the absence of her husband. If she survived the first husband, she could bring the business experience amassed during her first marriage into the second one. She could then lighten the workload of an ageing husband in the trading world and could, if necessary, act as his representative or at least keep the busi-

ness going with the help of an assistant, who was some-times a poor relative. Correspondence, account books, and wills passed down from the medieval traders all allow us to trace the gradual infiltration of the wife into the husband's business activities and into the realm of the family's interests.

The ledger of a Regensburg wholesale merchant, Matthias Runtinger (1383–1407), provides us with par-ticularly detailed information on this topic. His wife often acted as witness to sales deals and was responsible for small purchases of cloth, gold thread, and silk and, later, for basic bookkeeping. Her father-in-law there-after entrusted her with keeping records of individual business transactions when her husband was away on business trips. In this way she was gradually introduced to merchant business practices and to financial dealings and was increasingly able to represent her husband, who was already overburdened with duties in charge of the town. She was entrusted with the task of overseeing the registration of currency exchanges, which was always undertaken by an experienced employee.

Given the large number of different currencies in-volved, running the exchange office was a task that re-quired particular accuracy and reliability. Sometimes Runtinger's wife worked at the exchange desk. Likewise, when Lettel, their assistant, was away on a three- or four-week business trip to the Frankfurt trade fair, his own wife on at least one occasion took over this job. Runtinger's wife thus received a broad education in the family business and was able in the last years of her husband's life to take over and carry out the bookkeep-ing and business of the firm independently.

Another accounts book, that of Alexius Funck from Wiener Neustadt, shows that his wife also had consider-able business skills. After the death of her husband Mar-garete Funck carried on the wholesale trade business with the help of a steward, who was responsible for re-tail trade, and another assistant. For trade with Hungary she also employed someone with knowledge of the lan-guage, who did not 'live in' the household, but was

'from the streets of Vienna'. In 1524, however, after two and a half years of running the business independ-ently, she handed it over to the steward, who had been married to one of her husband's nieces for over six years.

According to the accounts of the Nuremberg mer-chant Hans Praun (1471–1478), his wife was also a reli-able business partner. She collected payments in his ab-sence, paid bills, received deliveries of goods, dealt with the craftsmen, and distributed small loans within the family network.

In Cologne, too, women formed trading companies with their husbands and on their death carried on busi-ness as usual. Such was the case with the widow Alheid de Rode, who carried out the company contract made with Lübeck wholesale traders for goods to be sent to Stockholm, Gotland, and Scania. Grietgen van der Burg of Cologne took over her husband's many business in-terests in Italy and his trade with Bruges, the trade with Italy being conducted through a company formed with Heinrich Vurberg and his wife Druidgen.

In 1508 a Basle couple, Hanns Rudolff Fryge and Ennel von Busch, formed a cloth company and swore to stand by it 'through profit and loss'. The conditions of the contract stated, among other things, that neither of the Fryges could lend any money made from the trading business without the knowledge of their Strasbourg partner. One clause covered the eventuality of both marriage partners being away on business trips, which suggests that the wife was on an equal footing.

A similar husband-wife business relationship was ap-parently formed by Michael Vischer, citizen of Völker-markt, and his wife. He was first a steward with the Nuremberg Behaim company and later an independent cloth merchant. The Behaim business papers twice men-tion business trips made by Mrs. Vischer. In 1455 she rode to St. Wolfgang, also carrying with her a letter from the Behaim brothers for Salzburg. In 1457, much to the regret of Martin Behaim, she moved with her husband to Laibach. Behaim wanted 250 guilders from her and knew that she kept her husband's accounts in Völkermarkt. He wanted to persuade her to return there, but knew she would object and considered going to Laibach to find her.

The legal pronouncements of the Magdeburg lay assessors from 1462 also mention the business partnership of a Görlitz couple. In order to pay back a woad debt of almost 100 marks, they had to mortgage two farmsteads. The Zwickau town council owed a Bamberg wine merchant couple 81 guilders. In the absence of her husband, Elisabeth Fyncke wrote the following receipt, dated 1459, for the Zwickau town council courier Nyclas Zopff, who had been sent to repay the debt: 'I, the aforementioned Elisabeth Fyncke, declare the aforementioned one and eighty guilders to have been settled by the aforementioned mayor and town council of Zwickau and all their successors, in my own name and that of my absent husband, the aforementioned Heintz Fyncke and all our successors. So we are quits once and for all'. In other central European towns—Mühlhausen in Thuringia, Judenburg in Austria, and Stade in northern Germany—women were familiar with their husbands' business affairs and as widows would carry on the trade.

A document in the Mühlhausen town archive, namely a letter of recommendation from Duchess Margaretha of Brunswick and Lüneburg, Countess of Henneberg, for Barbara Mauermann of Meiningen, provides an impressive illustration of how the widows who took over their partners' trading companies or the daughters who took over their fathers' trading companies or usury business did not always have an easy life. In this letter, dated 1482, the countess calls upon all her stewards, bailiffs, village mayors, tenant counts, mayors, councillors, and the rest of her subjects to give assistance to Linhart Isener, the relative and authorised representative of Barbara Mauermann, a citizen of Meiningen, in the collecting of debt payments within the countess' land. The reasoning used to explain why Linhart Isener rather than Barbara was being sent to collect the money

owed to her father is most interesting. The letter states: 'We, Margaretha born by the grace of God duchess of Brunswick and Lüneburg . . . wish to make public by way of this open letter, that one of our subjects in Meiningen, Barbara Mauermann, has explained to us that her deceased father Andreas Mauermann is due a considerable amount of money in the form of unpaid debts from debtors both within and beyond the boundaries of our land. Since she is, however, a member of the fairer sex and it is therefore not befitting for her to go everywhere herself to collect the unsettled debts, and since she cannot insist on payment in the same way as a man, she has most earnestly beseached us to allow the bearer of this letter . . . to locate, demand and receive repayment of all outstanding debts within and beyond the boundaries of our land'.[9]

The independent female merchant, like her male equivalent in the trading and financial world, had to show not just commitment and courage but a certain degree of skill, perseverance, and toughness. For this reason women from the upper stratum of town society who wanted to be independent often tried to find professions which were easier to master, which could be better combined with family obligations and societal norms, but which were nevertheless potentially quite profitable. This does not necessarily mean the making of bed linen and pieces of clothing for the household, which was usually left to the maids. In most of the European countries the women concerned themselves instead with beer brewing, or they ran a tavern where this highly popular drink was served, had an inn, traded in commissioned goods or in miscellaneous small goods, or ran pawn shops. The latter were usually run by Jewish women, who had been excluded from other professions. Some of the married women who decided to lead an independent professional life chose an activity different from that of their husbands. They devoted themselves to merchant trading, ran a brewery and tavern, or were active in the town bond market. The wives of permanently employed town officials, lawyers, or town clerks were also professionally active. From the end of the fifteenth century, during the transition to early forms of capitalist production, the concentration of various professions in the hands of married couples or of individual families led to the creation of firms that farmed out work, as was the case with the Cologne silk guild. Here the husband concerned himself with trade and the wife saw to the silk weaving. The married couple could in this way build up considerable economic power. They were able to make craftswomen dependent on them and eventually to employ them as wage labour. Among families from the upper stratum of town society the most common arrangement seems to have been for the husband, father, or son to be occupied in some aspect of wholesale trade, while the wife, daughter, or mother was concerned with small-scale retail trade. Independent commercial activity by the female members of the wealthy town bourgeoisie was encouraged by the fact that this was a way of exploiting profitable business opportunities as they arose, even when the husband had already specialised in some other profession. As with property ownership and bond acquisition, such female employment provided a safety net for families that were otherwise vulnerable to the risks involved in the world of trade and commerce.

The behaviour of one English lady, Margery Kempe from the town of Lynn, suggests that some women had different motives for choosing an independent professional life. Margery was married to one of the richest merchants in the town but herself ran first a brewery and then a mill. She claims that although she was the mother of fourteen children, she had enough time to have an independent commercial life. She admits, however, that she was also motivated by the wish to earn enough money to buy herself elegant clothes. Wives of the most well-to-do town burghers often found that their husbands would not give them enough money to dress themselves in a manner befitting the family's social position and compatible with the expectations of their class. Alessandra Macinghi, a member of the Florentine

Strozzi family, makes no secret of this in her letters. Showing marked disapproval of her son-in-law, she writes about the problems her eldest daughter had with her wardrobe: 'If Alessandra wants to darn her underskirt, then she has to pull her overdress over her blouse'.

* A popular trading activity in European towns with overseas trading and export interests both among unmarried women and married women or widows with an independent professional life was that of the small shopkeeper (institrix). This was a different occupation than that of the female wholesale trader or merchant (mercatrix). The difference is marked in some towns through the financial contribution required of members of the appropriate guilds. In Mühlhausen (Thuringia), for example, the membership fee was two marks for the merchant guild and one mark for the shopkeeper's guild. Occasionally the shopkeepers were also required to observe certain rules of behaviour and clothing regulations. Thus the Goslar shopkeeper law of 1281 states that a woman is subject to a small fine, to be paid to the mastercraftsman, should she leave the shop (in the case of the less well-off this was a small hut; for the better-off it was a vaulted room) without putting her coat on. Obviously the male shopkeepers were afraid that the reputation of the guild could be damaged by a lack of dress sense on the part of their female colleagues. Nor, it seems, were squabbles among the female shopkeepers tolerated by the guild, which was seemingly ever mindful of the profession's reputation. Female members involved in such internecine squabbles were subject to a fine of six small shillings, one of which had to be paid to the master, and five into the guild funds.

The male and female shopkeepers may well have shown an overall concern for the honour and reputation of their association, but they came from widely differing social positions. There is evidence that certain female shopkeepers occupied a highly respected social position. Thus in 1266 the burghers of Freiburg im Breisgau chose to meet in the house of the shopkeeper Frau von Herbotesheim when they wanted to discuss the legal bill of sale of an important building, a mill. It is also known that the wife of the Görlitz shopkeeper Hans Brückner went to the mayor's house and to the town hall in order to make the payments for the purchase of a well-known shop. She seems to have been a resolute lady who succeeded in looking after her own interests in the course of a further three marriages.

Some idea of the wealth amassed by individual female shopkeepers can be gleaned from wills, marriage contracts, and land and other tax registers. Thus in Lübeck we find the will of Mechthild von Bremen, which is dated 14 April 1353. Apart from clothing and jewellery, she left behind 30 marks in cash and other indeterminate goods in the hands of the executors. Another female shopkeeper's will, likewise from Lübeck, is dated 16 June 1359. It refers to financial bequests worth up to 51 marks. Grete von Revele left all her mobile and immobile property to her husband. It is interesting to compare this with the will of the female merchant Alheyd von Bremen, the wife of Vico Wittenborch. She does not have much more clothing than the aforementioned shopkeepers (two dresses and one underskirt) but on the other hand has valuable jewellery, silver cutlery, and a house; and she has lent her husband 400 marks of her own money which he had not paid back. But she had less ready cash than the shopkeepers and could therefore only make bequests to the value of 15 marks. The widow of a Görlitz shopkeeper by the name of Hans Brückner had—as was often the case in medieval towns—previously invested most of her father's fortune in a small general store for her husband. On his death she then inherited the whole fortune. Apart from this there were some legacies to third persons which were covered by outstanding debts. In the common will she had drawn up with her second husband, she was entitled to 100 marks and very probably used them for her own independent trading activity. This is suggested by the clause which states that she

would like to leave her husband everything she possessed and would earn in the future. This formulation was common in the case of businessmen who named their wives sole heir. Tax lists and registers indicate that the female shopkeepers ranked fairly high among the property-owning town inhabitants. For example, the tax books in Basle for the year 1429 list 30 tax-paying female shopkeepers. A report of the theft, near Beinheim, of goods from a train of pack-horses and two-wheeled carts is also revealing with regard to the activities of the female shopkeepers in Switzerland. Of the 61 shopkeepers adversely affected by the theft—that is, who were expecting deliveries from the goods train—37 were women. Among those who suffered particularly high losses were a certain Cristina Oflaterin (501 guilders) and the widow of a chemist (270 guilders). Other female shopkeepers expected smaller amounts of goods worth between $7^1/_2$ and 9 guilders. Female shopkeepers are also listed among the taxpayers in Mühlhausen in Thuringia. The register of this town, which was opened in 1400, mentions a widow who was entitled to membership in the shopkeepers' guild and who, due to her considerable fortune, had to pay an annual tax contribution of $71^1/_2$ marks.

The main difference between the merchant and the shopkeeper was to be found in the structure of each of their business activities. The mercatrix bought and sold wholesale goods—wine, cloth, dyes, wool, metal goods, spices, etc. The shopkeeper invested her fortune in a wider selection of goods which she used to satisfy the demand of local customers and those in the often extensive surrounding market.

The Erfurt regulations for male and female membership in the shopkeepers' guild, published in 1486, permit the sale of the following assortment of goods: spices, herbs, tropical and subtropical fruits, paper, cotton, fustian, linen, *Harras* (woven woollen ribbon), velvet, silk, linen from foreign countries, Venetian liquorice, crude gold, and silver. Probably in order to quash any competition from small traders, these goods could be delivered only to and from the shopkeepers' bridge. The following selection of goods was permitted in the town and on the bridge: juniper berries, field cumin, dyes, pine soot, raisins, millet, brimstone (large and small), wooden jugs, Flemish yarn, sandalwood, corals, silk bonnets, Bohemian black ribbon, Frankfurt ribbon, and Nuremberg ribbon.

The goods listed come almost exclusively under the category of so-called dry goods, as opposed to perishable goods. These were also the goods on offer from the female shopkeepers in, for example, Cologne and Worms. The Görlitz shopkeepers had a similar range of wares. Our knowledge of this town concerning the first third of the fifteenth century is particularly good due to its involvement in the Hussite wars, and it seems that, because of its political background, there were several exceptions to the rule. All provide evidence of how the female shopkeepers reacted to market demand. During the period

when the town council was involved in anti-Hussite war activities the Görlitz women had on offer a range of goods that, judging from the town accounts, were totally geared to wartime needs: Arras woollen cloth, ticking and various types of linen suitable for banners and flags used in army campaigns, buckets and spades, powder sieves, cord and tools for the wagon workshop, and canvas for nosebags, cribs, and cart awnings.

The range of wares on offer from a female shopkeeper by the name of Czachmannin, who supplied the Görlitz town council from 1409 to 1431, included the following items: crossbow covers, saddlebags, bridles, belts, spurs, stirrups, holsters, breast straps, brimstone, copperas, verdigris, quivers, soap, parchment, wax, paper, and spices.

The account book of Hans Brückner of Görlitz, which dates from 1476 to 1496 and which informs us of his wife's involvement in the business, presents a picture of a selection of wares more geared toward peacetime needs. The

A female trader, who presumably sells pawned goods, accepts a man's gown. Woodcut, printed by Hans Hofmann, Nuremberg, 1490. In: Albert Schramm, *Der Bilderschmuck der Frühdrucke.* Vol. XVIII. Leipzig, 1935, ill. 647.

following items illustrate the wide range of goods: wheat-beer, flax, pearls, paper, candles, black fustian, bay leaves, almonds, peach kernels, draperies, soap, oil, dyed skins, bath basins, clocks, mirrors, books (bibles, almanacs, Lombard tales, Latin postils), candle snuffers, shoe soles, and bags. Beer, flax and soap seem to have been sold particularly frequently or in particularly large quantities.

In the case of the Funck family from Wiener Neustadt, the Runtingers in Regensburg, Karyssa under Helmslegern in Cologne, and the Brückners in Görlitz, wholesale and retail trade often seem to have been concentrated in the same business. The distinction between the (male or female) merchant and the shopkeeper must be made ultimately by deciding which aspect of their trade—wholesale or retail—was predominant in their commercial activities. The distinction is fine, especially because the shopkeepers' guild provided a sort of safety net for unsuccessful merchants.

The profile of all the large European merchant trading towns is marked not least by the presence of a large number of small traders and pedlars, many of whom were also women. Because even those with a low income could set up in business in the various branches of small trade, many women chose to do so as a supplementary or even main source of income. This step was made even easier due to the lack of guilds for small traders within Europe. The women could thus avoid the often unfavourable guild regulations. As far as the small traders in groceries were concerned, it was only in some of the Hanseatic League towns, such as Lübeck, Stade and Lüneburg, that they were organised in guilds.

It was not difficult, then, to set up as a small trader; but the chances of making one's fortune, at least in a legal manner, were on the whole small. In tax lists street traders are often entered as 'nothing but hearth tax' *(nichil praeter larem)* or are absolved from tax payment with the remark 'possess nothing' *(nichil habent)*. In an early Italian print dating from the fifteenth century, women are represented waiting with their goods for buyers but also sitting with a spindle, which would suggest that they could

not live from either of these occupations alone. This was almost certainly true for most saleswomen (*Keuflerin, Keufel* in German; *regrattières* in French), who resold goods or often only a few of each article in return for a small fixed mark-up on the original price. According to a Nuremberg and an Ulm council regulation dating from the fourteenth century, as well as court records from Mühlhausen in Thuringia, salesmen and women seem sometimes out of sheer poverty to have pawned their goods. In the Nuremberg decree they are instructed to give back the income for the sold goods to the buyer and not to 'borrow or keep it' overnight. In some towns saleswomen even seem to have been allowed to deal in used goods only. Thus a Breslau regulation on shopkeepers (undated) forbids them to sell new things apart from on market day. Some, however, did succeed in making a small fortune. This made it possible for them to pay the usual deposit to the town council in order to become a registered saleswoman and in this capacity to sell on behalf of a creditor the second-hand goods submitted in lieu of payment.

Most of the small trade, however, was undoubtedly concentrated in the hands of those male and female retail traders who specialised in certain goods, catering to the daily needs of the town population and the local market.

A fifteenth-century legal document tells us that there were about 45 female traders in the town of Ofen, two-thirds of whom were German, the rest Hungarian. These women had permission to sell fruit, vegetables, poultry, cheese, game, and herbs. The fruit trader sold cherries, strawberries, plums and sloes, apples, pumpkins, peaches, green nuts and almonds as well as dried fruit. The vegetable seller had pulses, millet, barley, fennel, and dried garlic on offer; the herb trader fresh greens, parsley, carrots, and spinach. The wives of the baker, butcher, fishman, purse maker, belt maker, candle maker, and smith also supplied the town market with goods from their own production.

* If we want to draw a clearer distinction between wholesale trader, small shopkeeper, and small trader,

we have to look at the differences in their training and way of conducting business. In English medieval towns, the female merchant was apparently required to have a seven-year training, but this was certainly not required of female shopkeepers, who also had fewer possibilities to employ agents to settle their affairs outside the local market.

Business accounts were kept in more detail and with greater precision by the female merchants, probably because of the more sophisticated education given to those from the middle stratum of the town or from the patrician upper stratum. However, the female shopkeepers also required some sort of record of their trade activities, however simple. The records from Cologne are particularly informative on this score. We are given clear information about the trade book of a Cologne lady by the name of Ailheyd von Dryveltz thanks to a letter dated 15 November 1471 from the town of Cologne to the town of Diest. This letter refers to a thick accounts book bound in leather in which she wrote all her demands for outstanding debts, especially for wine.

After the death of Ailheyd von Dryveltz (born before 1455) her business accounts book was used by the executors of her will to collect money due to her from customers in Brabant, Liège, Laon, Flanders, Holland, and Zealand. Accounts books dating from around 1500 were kept by Elss Lynenweiffers, the cloth merchant Dorothea Venlo, and Niesgin Yss of Cologne. The accounts book of Fygin von Syburg, dating from 1475 to approximately 1490, has been preserved to this day. She traded largely in cloth.

It was by no means unusual for women to make business trips, whether they were money lenders, wholesale traders, wives of merchants, small storekeepers, retail traders, or wives of craftsmen. The aforementioned letter from the town of Danzig to the English town of Lynn tells us that a lady citizen of Danzig made several business trips to England. Due to the unreliability of her English agent in Lynn, who had not passed on the money given to him for rented horses, she ran into difficulties and asked the town council of Danzig for support, in order not to have her reputation as a good and honest businesswoman tarnished. The wife of a certain wholesale trader, Pengel of Strasbourg, managed his financial affairs in Vienna. The Frankfurt trade fair was frequented by a female silk trader or shopkeeper from Lusatia as well as by numerous lady merchants or small traders from Cologne. The Cologne female silk makers also attended regularly at the end of the fifteenth century. Ladies from that city were also to be spotted at the Antwerp trade fair and undertook business trips to the Netherlands. The female fish merchants of Cologne sold their wares in Bingen and Mainz. One lady from Esslingen collected debts in Stuttgart, a lady from Magdeburg tried to claim an inheritance in Erfurt, and a lady from Cologne travelled with both her sons to Leipzig for a similar purpose.

These journeys were not without their dangers. Thus the Queen of Denmark laments in a letter to the town council of Stralsund that the wife of a Copenhagen citizen had been taken prisoner in Stralsund. 'On the highroad of the Empire', probably on the way to the Frankfurt trade fair, a lady from Mühlhausen was held up and robbed. The same thing happened to another Cologne citizen, the widow of Ludwig von Kasel, who was taken prisoner with her servants. There were similar incidents recorded in 1442 and 1502 concerning women who were travelling on business on behalf of their husbands; the list could be continued indefinitely.

* Women who engaged in trade and financial matters were granted certain legal concessions in municipal law from quite an early date. Italy was the first to offer such concessions, with Lombard law allowing various exceptions to the husband's right of guardianship over his wife. In the Italian maritime towns a prospering economy created conditions conducive to the further relaxation of the law. In these towns unmarried women had the exclusive right to dispose of their own property as they wished and even married women had extensive

rights with regard to their husbands' property. This can be seen, for example, in the fact that women could be appointed as executors of wills in the early thirteenth century, a ruling which did not apply in the part of Europe north of the Alps at least until the late Middle Ages. However, even in northern Europe, concurrent with the granting of town charters, some legal autonomy had been conceded to the merchant women as early as the eleventh century and was extended in the town statutes of the thirteenth and fourteenth centuries.

The first step was to abolish the limitations on the merchant woman's legal right to dispose of her own property. The general rule for female town inhabitants was that they could have only a small amount of money at their disposal, unless their husband or guardian allowed them more. The actual amount of money they were entitled to varied from town to town: in Mühlhausen (Thuringia), it was the value of the woman's headdress—that is, 6 pfennigs; in Lübeck 2½ shillings; and in Freiburg im Breisgau 4 denarii. The merchant woman was conceded to be an exception and this position was consolidated in the course of the development of the towns.

Early evidence of this special status is provided by the Augsburg town law of 1276, where it is stated: 'No woman has the right to give someone else a part of her husband's estate, neither as surety nor in any other form without her husband's consent, unless she has her own business, run from her own shop or cellar or she is involved in trading activity independent of her husband; neither may a woman take any matter to court without her husband's permission . . . unless she goes to the market and buys and sells'. . . . The right of economically independent women to take grievances to court is also given express recognition in the Goslar town law of 1330/1350. In the Lübeck town law of 1294, the merchant woman's equality with men before the law is formulated as follows: 'No maiden, wife, nor widow may sell her estate nor give it away, nor lend it . . . unless they have a selling place, in which case they are as finan-

cially self-accountable as men'.[10] In other words, the merchant woman could freely dispose of her own estate, but she was also solely responsible for her own debts. The Lübeck citizen Alheyd von Bremen has left us a testimony of her full legal trading rights in her will, dated 18 November 1358. From the very start she emphasises that in practising the profession of merchant (mercatura) she has no guardian and has never had one. She is a merchant who buys and sells independently. She has accepted her husband into her property (ad possessionem meam).

The town council of Strasbourg showed exceptional understanding for the plight of the unmarried or widowed merchant woman. When a clause to the effect that citizens had to be home—except for absences of one or two nights—from Martinmas to Candlemas (the tax-collecting period) was included in the town law of 1322, female citizens absent on business trips were expressly exempted from this obligation. They did, however, have to leave their children and their servants in the town.

English medieval town law guaranteed legal trading freedom to the independent merchant woman, albeit in a roundabout way. Due to stronger links established at this time between the towns in England and affairs of the kingdom, the husband's rights as guardian were strengthened rather than weakened, and the towns had to grant the married woman equal legal status with unmarried women in order to allow them to be independently employed. Thus, for example, the town law of Lincoln states that if a woman practises a trade that her husband has nothing to do with, she should be treated as a single woman in all matters concerning it.

Whether overtly or covertly, directly or indirectly, legal norms began to be accepted, first in merchant law, which led to a visible improvement in the legal position of the professionally active woman. This development took place against the background of an economically flourishing town life in Europe, the towns being already partially free of feudal rule. Male legal rights as guardians over women, which had been firmly anchored in feudal law, were gradually eroded. The town councils, dominated by merchants, incorporated the new legal principles into municipal law and set about dealing with all the implications of this transferal—for the rules on the husband and wife's shared responsibility for debt repayments and the security of the wife's dowry should her husband fall into debt; division of property and in extreme cases divorce due to proven business malpractice on the part of the husband; and the relaxation of the merchant woman's legal obligation to be present in her home town during the tax-collecting period.

The legal backing given to the tradeswoman helped considerably to increase her sense of responsibility and independence, whether in dealings with trade partners, her husband, her family, or the town community. In this way the joint activities of husband and wife in west and central European trade and export centres strengthened the merchants as an economically influential group, in the interests of both the merchant-dominated town councils and the great feudal lords who were especially interested in improving the internal structures of their territories.

Women in the Crafts and Other Town Trades

The development of the town economy was not limited to trade alone but was also closely bound up with the specialisation and intensification of craft production. And since trade stimulated the demographic growth of the towns, new demands began to be made in the inn-keeping and services sector, medical and social services, town administration, and construction. The complex network of trade and cultural links between towns with economies based on either long-distance trade, export, or mining, and the corresponding increase in the obligations and duties of the prosperous burghers, further stimulated the cultural needs and educational aspirations of town dwellers. What was the situation with the other professions, those not connected with merchant trading, in the medieval European town? Did their growth encourage the professional employment of women to the same extent that the economic development of the towns and their partial liberation from the rule of the feudal town lords did?

* In the case of merchants we had such obvious and informative sources as account books and business letters. This is not the case for the town craftworker. Neither do wills offer such detailed information. There are various reasons for this: the majority of the craftsmen, in order to remain competitive, had to draw on the labour of the whole family—for work in the house and workshop and for selling their products—and could hardly benefit from the increase in secular educational opportunities that occurred from the thirteenth century onward. On the other hand, it was not necessary for them to keep regular or strict accounts due to their modest turnover and limited circle of customers. In the official town legislation, which, with few exceptions, usually reflected the interests of the patrician and merchant strata, craftworkers and those working in other trades are given scant attention, being mentioned only in the context of guild legislation or in a list of their obligations in terms of services they had to provide to the town. The customs and laws of the craft guilds do, however, provide an extremely important form of source material and are revealing with regard to the living conditions of the craft families. They outline the legal conditions for women's participation in the crafts. In other words, they sketch the potential for women in this sphere, but they do not, unfortunately, permit us to estimate the extent to which this potential was exploited. The guild legislation was, moreover, mainly concerned with explaining such rules and customs which experience had shown were not automatically respected and which might, therefore, cause conflict. In short, as a source, the official guild legislation is not sufficient: to gain a picture that corresponds more closely to historical reality, it has to be supplemented by sources that provide a picture of how legal regulations were actually interpreted in daily life. These supplementary sources are provided above all by the rich archival material recording the sentences passed in court proceedings. The town and court records contain reports of court sentences for offences against property, the premature ending of employment,

complaints with regard to outstanding wage payments, compensation for medical costs and failure to pay wages, apprentice contracts, and so on. Such sources are just beginning to be explored and analysed.

We have very rich and informative sources for the capital of France, a country in which feudalism developed in a particularly typical fashion. The 'Book of Trades' *(Livre des métiers)*, drawn up and edited by the royal judge, Etienne Boileau, in 1270, probably on the order of King Louis IX (1226–1270), contains descriptions of the duties and rights of 100 Parisian craft guilds. The extent to which the trades listed in this book were actually practised can be roughly gauged by making a comparison with the Paris tax registers *(Livres de la taille)* of 1292, 1300, and 1313, which also list the number of independent working women. The woman's profession is frequently different from that of her husband. These registers are not totally reliable, since they cover only those crafts that were organised by a guild. Not all the professions practised by women had a guild organisation, and the actual number of professional women was therefore probably higher than the tax register tallys.

Bearing in mind the limitations of the Paris sources, we can still draw certain conclusions from them with regard to female occupations. One of the oldest practised exclusively by women in Paris was the beating, teasing, and carding of flax and hemp for textile making. The production of linen yarn took place in a mixed guild, with both men and women workers. Apprentices of both sexes had to undergo a six-year training. Flax and hemp spinning was also carried out in a mixed guild. It probably dated from the late thirteenth century, since Philip VI pronounced his approval of its constitution in 1349. The tax registers of 1292 and 1300 list 11 representatives of this profession, but do not state whether they are male or female. Likewise it is impossible to determine the proportion of female members and the position of the female members in the linen-weavers' guild that existed in Paris at the end of the thirteenth century.

There are 2 female wool spinners entered in the 1292 tax register under the auxiliary trades for woollen cloth production and 2 female woolworkers and 1 female carder in the 1300 registers. Among the clothmakers themselves, widows were the only women to have the status of master. This tallies with the number of women entered in the 1300 tax list: there were only 10 women compared to 350 men.

It was normal in the textile trades for women to help their husbands. The work of the cloth fuller, however, was so physically strenuous that the guild actually forbade the fullers' wives to help with their husbands' work. Widows were allowed to carry on their husbands' trade with the help of two apprentices and the children from the first or later marriages. But judging from the tax registers they do not seem to have made use of this right.

Women masters or workers were also a rarity among feltmakers. The 1300 tax register is the only one that mentions two female feltmakers *(feutrières)*. On the other hand, the ribbon- and braid-weaving guild, which incorporated members working with silk, twirl, wool, and cotton, had numerous female masters who could also be responsible for the training of apprentices. Widows of masters could carry on their trade independently, and since the tax registers of 1292 and 1300 list only 9 women and no men, it can be assumed that unmarried women were also allowed to work in this craft. On the other hand, men dominated the crafting of gold ribbon until the beginning of the fourteenth century. (This probably involved the beating of gold and production of a fine gold-leaf.) By 1400 the guild had almost doubled its membership and included 27 male and female masters, but the proportions are not known.

The Paris silk-manufacturing trade, which flourished until the late fifteenth century, produced some sizeable guilds that were an exclusively female domain. This was the time of the two separate silk-spinner guilds: one for those using large spindles and one for those using the smaller ones which produced stronger thread. The silk spinners using the big spindles were professionally independent in every sense. They had the right to take on and train apprentices and to employ in their workshops their own children as well as the children of their husband's previous marriages. The husbands were obviously employed in different professions. The exclusively female guild had two male overseers who were commissioners from the town council (prud'hommes jurés). The guild for the small spindle silk spinners was open to men. According to its statutes, apprentices of both sexes could be trained in the craft over a period of seven years. This craft association seems to have been overseen by two male masters and two specially appointed women from the trade (preudesfames du mestier). Activities such as apprentice training could be supervised by female journeymen. In practice, however, the craft of silk spinning with small spindles seems to have been an exclusively female occupation. The 1292 tax register contains a joint entry for the tax payments of both the spinning guilds. The tax payers in this register include 8 female silk spinners; in the 1300 register, 36.

The number of tax-paying female silk weavers was also relatively high and they too formed an exclusively female guild. In order to be granted the title of master in this guild, a woman had to complete an apprenticeship successfully and practise the trade for one year with a spotless record. The guild was supervised by 3 male masters and 3 female masters (maîtresses-jurées). It is strange, however, that the tax register for the year 1300 lists 38 female journeymen (ouvrières de soie) and only 1 female (master) silk cloth producer. The category ouvrières de, female workers in such and such a trade, is often met in the source material and corresponds to a female journeyman, a term used in several senses in the Middle Ages. The strange disproportion between 1 female master and 38 female journeymen in the tax register can only be explained if one surmises that some rich female silk producers paid their taxes all in one go, handing over large sums of money to the council for this purpose, or that some female masters had large debts, which meant that they were incapable of paying taxes. Both of these suppositions are feasible in medieval European towns.

The Paris purse-makers' guild (faiseuses d'aumendières sarrazinoises) was another purely female organisation. Like the silk makers they were also obliged to complete a year as journeyman after the apprenticeship training before they could become masters. This was unusual for the time (thirteenth century), although it became the norm later on, in the fifteenth century. Finally, the silk hat makers is another example of a Parisian female guild. Paris also had a series of mixed guilds in which men and women could be masters with equal rights—the embroidery, pearl hat-maker, and yarn-maker guilds.

The female guilds all represented trades which required, apart from taste and a sense of fashion, a certain manual dexterity, particularly given the relatively underdeveloped level of the equipment used. The granting to women of the right to form their own guild was enough to stimulate female participation in this trade and must have had an overall positive influence on the quality of the goods produced.

Widows had the right to occupy the position of master in the butcher, pancake-baker, fishmonger, baker, rosarymaker, bagmaker, hatmaker, beltmaker, leathercrafter (cordouaniers), cutler, glass-grinder, tailor, and dyer trades. Of the 321 professions to be found within the trade and crafts sector of the second half of the thirteenth and early fourteenth centuries, and which are known due to the Paris Livre des métiers and tax register, 108 were practised by women, either as widows of masters, independent masters, wives of masters, journeymen, or apprentices. Apart from this, numerous serving girls were taken on as untrained labour when the workload required extra hands. Since Paris was the royal residence and the country's administrative centre, women were also employed to satisfy the various requirements of the court. The elevated status of these women can be guessed at from the legal sentences passed by the royal court.

It would certainly be misleading to make generalisations about the rest of Europe on the basis of the impressively independent work activity of the Paris women and their participation in the production of craft goods and services within the overall framework of the guilds. Paris was a royal residence, a city with a tradition of trading, business, and academic links with the rest of the world. Also, with a population of almost 80,000 in the fourteenth century, there was a high level of demand for craft goods in general, as well as for luxury goods, groceries, skilled services, and manpower. Even the less well-off had plenty of opportunities to acquire a modest level of training or education. Thus the possibilities for the female inhabitants of the city to be active in certain crafts and to produce them independently were unusual, and marked the peak of what could be achieved with regard to female professional work within the medieval town guilds of western and central Europe.

In the English guilds, the attitude toward women compared badly with that of the Paris guilds, which on the whole had a positive effect on the position of women in the economic life of the town. In England it was, in some cases, strictly forbidden to take on women as auxiliary workers unless they were wives of a master or her maid. This was the case, for example, in the first half of the fourteenth century in the London belt-maker guild or in the second half of the fifteenth century for the weavers' guild in Bristol. The cloth fullers of Lincoln demanded in about 1297 that no one should work in the craft except the wife of the master or her maid. Yet because of demands made on craft production in everyday English town life, the strict rules limiting female participation were not always observed. Wills show that craftsmen left money—among other things—for the professional training of their daughters. The wife of a London cutler had to swear in 1364 that she would provide her girl apprentice with clothing and not punish her with a stick or a knife. London silk producers also had apprentice contracts. They have not been organised in a guild, but whenever a matter such as foreign competition posed a threat to their craft, they would arrange agreements and in 1368 and 1455 even managed to arrange royal audiences. On these occasions, they argued in the following vein: 'Sheweth unto your great wisdoms and also prayen and beseechen the Silkwomen and Throwstres of the Crafts and occupation of silkwork w'in the City of London, which be and have been crafts of women w'in the same city of time that no mind runneth to the contrary—that where upon the same crafts, before this time, many a worshipful woman within the city have lived full honourably and therewith many good households kept and many gentlewomen and others in great number like as there be more than 1000, have been drawn under them in learning the same crafts and occupation full virtuously under the plesaunce of God, whereby afterwards they have grown to great worship'.[11]

Until relatively recent times, the reputation of an honourable woman in western and central Europe depended to a large extent on whether she could provide her family and her house with textiles, clothes, and other necessities. Thus we can safely assume that the above-mentioned 'noblewomen and many others' learned to work with silk not in order to make their living from the trade but to enhance their reputation as lady of the house or as potential marriage candidates.

The fact that the guild legislation in England did less to promote female work than that in other developed European countries, and that it was particularly unfavourable with regard to women working independently as masters, can be explained partly in economic and partly in political terms. Since the fourteenth century, wool, England's main export item, had been processed largely in rural textile centres, which had developed rapidly thanks to royally backed Flemish immigration. The old guild towns, on the other hand, went into decline. Their guilds lacked economic drive and thus the motivation to react in a positive way to the new demands of international trade. They remained conservative. The political situation in English towns thus diverged from that in Italian, French, and German towns. They remained firmly under the control of certain feudal lords or the king and as a result the guilds of London, for example, were dependent on the king and his officials.

One consequence of this conservative attitude on the part of the guilds was that the female inhabitants took on several subsidiary jobs. Many were forced by circumstances to contribute to the family income, to provide for the family alone, or simply to look out for themselves. William Langland describes such a woman, Rose, the wife of Avarice, in his *Piers Plowman*: 'My wife was a weaver and woollen cloth made. She spake to the spinners to spinnen it out. . . . I bought her barley malt, she brew it to sell. . . . Rose the Regrater was her right name. She hath holden huckstery all her life time'.[12]

The royal kingdom itself provided a certain amount of protection for professional female labour. A 1363 statute states: 'But the intent of the King and his Council is that Women, that is to say Brewers, Bakers, Carders, Spinners and Workers as well of Wool as of Linen Cloth and of Silk, Brawdesters and Breakers of Wool and all other that do use and work all handy works may freely use and work as they have done before this time without any impeachment or being restrained by this Ordinance'.[13] Such regulations were primarily to the advantage of the developing system of early capitalism in the textile trade and thus against the interests of the English town guilds, which were doomed to decline.

From the end of the thirteenth century to the second half of the fifteenth century independent female activity in the crafts became widely established in a number of western and central European maritime trade and export centres—the large towns of northern France, Flanders, northern Italy, the Rhine, southern and central Germany, Austria, Switzerland, and, to a lesser extent, in Poland and Bohemia. This development even spread to the medium-sized trade and manufacturing towns and also the smaller towns, whenever at least one branch of trade managed to specialise in export goods. It was usually the textile trade which did this.

* It tended to be the producers of clothing and luxury goods that formed guilds with free entry for women as apprentices, journeymen, and masters. These included the hemp-, linen-, and wool-processing trades—those who made rope, haircloth, cloth, towels, veils, braids, gloves, and hats; tailors, furriers, and saddle and purse makers; the belt makers; and gold-thread spinners and silk embroiderers.

One of the earliest guild organisations to grant equal rights to men and women was that of the furriers in Basle in the year 1226. Once they were members of the guild, women were allowed to work, buy, and sell in the same way as men. Women were also equal members of the furriers' guilds in Cologne, Frankfurt on Main, Regensburg, Lübeck, and Quedlinburg; and they were subject to the same regulations for the practice of the trade as the male members. Female inhabitants in the towns of Florence, Frankfurt on Main, Nuremberg, Munich, Mainz, Speyer, Cologne, Erfurt, Mühlhausen in Thuringia, and Nordhausen were active in the leather-processing trades—in the production of belts, purses, saddles, shoes, and parchment. In 1423 the guilds of Nuremberg, Munich, Mainz, Speyer, Frankfurt on Main, Basle, Worms, Fritzlar, and Strasbourg got together to formulate a ruling on the parchment trade, which gives permission in principle for the female inhabitants to practise the trade. The permission does not, however, extend to those women who marry outside the parchment trade: a clause designed to prevent individual guild members from enjoying economic advantages. Although the town of Erfurt was in no way affected by this joint agreement between southwest German towns, the Erfurt town council passed a ruling on their own town parchment trade in 1427 which forbade one female member to continue practising because she had married a man who was of a different trade and came from a different town, carrying out his business in Arnstadt. The Erfurt woman was banned from practising the parchment trade as long as her husband lived in Arnstadt and had a house and property there. The female felt hat producers in Lübeck got full rights as members of the guild organisations during the fourteenth century, those of Frankfurt on Main in 1407.[14] In the Nuremberg regulations of 1398, 1400, 1417, and 1420 the widows of hat makers are mentioned; each year, there was one female master, and in 1430 there were two.

According to the public records of Strasbourg, in the years 1445–1469, among various women given citizens' rights there were 3 who had the obligation to serve in the guild of the clothmakers and cloth shearers. In 1334 there were already 39 unmarried women and widows who were members of the Strasbourg wool-weaver and clothmaker guild. The town council in 1330 had already decided that women who weave woollen cloth or cotton cloth or loom cloth or employ a lad had to be members of the weavers' guild. Lists of members and contracts of the Strasbourg clothmaker guild contain 37 female names for the years 1400–1434. These women were, in all probability, active as independent masters within the cloth-producing trade. They included some dyers and some glove makers. In the fourteenth century, both sexes could also be members of the wool-weavers' guild of Frankfurt on Main. They are mentioned in the wool-weaver decree of 1377 (dyers and wool or yarn spinners came under the umbrella of this guild). The constitution of the Hamburg wool-weavers' guild, which dates from the first half of the fifteenth century, permitted only the widows of masters to enjoy the rights of a master, so long as they had no sons and did not remarry. In Munich and Stuttgart there was a guild for the whole weaving trade, and female masters of the three types of weaving in the town—wool, veil, and linen—were admitted. Apart from a few towns, such as Hamburg and Munich, it was usually the case in Germany that veil, fustian, and linen weaving remained outside the guild organisations until the fifteenth century, when guild membership became compulsory in these branches of the textile trade in, for example, Frankfurt on Main, Hildesheim, Ulm, Duderstadt, Neuss, and Strasbourg.

All these guilds were dependent on women's involvement. This was officially recognized in the masters' regulations of Munich, Frankfurt on Main, Stuttgart, Strasbourg, Hamburg (limited to the so-called small work), and Ulm, as long as the woman and her children had been citizens of the town for five years 'with house and goods'. In Neuss the linen weavers received statutes, which were obviously designed to promote women's independent work within the trade, since single women in the linen-weaving trade were entitled to a 50-percent reduction in the guild membership fee. The statutes also permitted the masters to take on their wives and children as apprentices. This must certainly have consolidated the position of the master's wife within the trade. Should she be widowed, she could be sure of being recognized as a fully qualified master. According to the sources, in the Ghent textile trade too, the husband had the right to train his wife. In the medium-sized merchant and manufacturing towns, where there was probably more fear of competition from lower-paid female labour than in the big trading and manufacturing centres, it was more difficult for women to be active in the trades. Sources relating to the history of Bamberg, Trier, Mühlhausen (Thuringia), Zwickau, and Chemnitz hint at maids being employed in the trades; there is less evidence of independent female masters, other than widows of masters in the textile trade.

Before we turn to the subject of female labour in other trades, it is worth pausing for a moment to consider the position of women in the Cologne textile trade, since it is particularly well covered by historical documents and research. The textile trade was one of the most important branches of the medieval trades in Cologne. 'Women were well represented in the textile guilds and their subsidiary trades and the very nature of this trade served to promote female employment. They did here in an organised manner what they had had to do for centuries: spinning, weaving, bleaching, wool carding, burling and similar work'.[15] Yarn and silk were produced exclusively by women. They had the rigth to belong to the linen-weaving and the fustian- and blanket-weaving guilds. On the other hand, independent female masters seem to have been the exception in the cloth-cutting, wool-weaving, and dying guilds. Generally, as we have mentioned, the right to be a master was limited to masters' widows, who were allowed to carry on the trade with a boy helper. The Cologne tailor trade also belonged to the textile-processing sector in a broader sense. Widows, daughters, and wives of masters were admitted to the tailors' guild. Others were permitted to take on female apprentices without leaving their status of seamstresses. Thus the Cologne tailors were subject to employment restrictions that were not observed in other large towns, such as Lübeck and Frankfurt on Main, or even in medium-sized towns, such as Siegburg and Überlingen. The drastic employment restrictions for female tailors were laid down in a 1426 town council decision, which was followed by a similar council decree in 1440. This actually suggests that these restrictions were difficult to implement. According to the decree, women were only allowed to remodel old petticoats or produce new ones made of patterned fustian or light material. The seamstresses were strictly excluded from the production of silk or woollen clothes, which would have been a much more lucrative occupation. Similar restrictions on female employment are found for the seamstresses of the town of Constance at the beginning of the second half of the fifteenth century. The Mainz tailors' guild's book of regulations dating from 1369 to 1447 gives us reason to believe that in fact the guild rules were, in practice, subject to the individual interpretation of the masters. This was true of the membership fee and the way in which this was paid; also of the permissible volume of work and the right to train female apprentices.

Despite certain restrictions on female labour in some branches of the textile trade, female guilds were formed in both Cologne and Paris. Particular mention should be made of the female yarn-makers' guild, which came into existence between 1370 and 1397. Cologne yarn—

'a linen thread, which was usually dyed blue and was distinguished by the way it was treated and finished and by the trueness of its colour'[16]—was a quality item for which there was international demand. The female yarn makers who formed the guild finished the linen, which had already been prepared by the twisters. Strict control ensured that no one mixed extraneous yarn (Erfurt yarn is mentioned frequently) with the native yarn.

According to an official charter dating from 1397, the size of the craft workshops was determined in such a way that every female master could introduce only one of her daughters to the guild. The mother, as master, was allowed to employ three female apprentices or waged workers trained in the profession, but the official charter allowed the daughter to employ only two such workers. In addition, the independent yarn maker could have the fabric processed outside her home over a period of fourteen days (with the possibility of an extension on this time limit).

The gold spinners were a part of the goldsmith trade that specialised in the production of fine thread through the beating and stretching of gold and silver. Metal threads made from gold, silver, silver-coated copper, or leather coated with metal were used immediately for weaving or were passed on to the gold spinners to be mixed with a base thread of silk, linen, or cotton. A tribute to the quality of the Cologne gold thread, which could be identified by a special marking, is provided by the fact that, in 1382, the highly developed silk trade in the northern Italian town of Lucca forbade the use of foreign silk or other materials for the production of its materials but made an exception in the case of the Cologne gold and silver thread—which was expressly called for in the most exclusive types of brocade. Like the yarn makers, the gold spinners and gold beaters were granted a guild charter. And as with the yarn makers, an attempt was made to create equal opportunities for the members of the guild through a ruling on the size of workshops. Unmarried female gold spinners were allowed to take on four girl helpers. If a female gold spinner was married to a gold beater, her husband was allowed to employ three girl spinners to help her.

A female guild was also formed within the Cologne silk trade, which dates from the mid-thirteenth century. The female silk-maker guild was called the *Seidamt* (silk office) in local dialect. This guild was formed in 1437 and originally incorporated the silk spinners, before they were granted their own guild organisation in 1456.

The silk trade included the silk dyers and two other specialised categories which were particularly important in attracting foreign trade: the silk embroiderers, who mainly produced liturgical garments, bishops' mitres, and ladies' bonnets (Cologne *ransen*), and the heraldic embroiderers. According to the official charter of 1397, men and women had equal rights as members of the guild of heraldic embroiderers.

The guild charters and supplementary rulings on all female and mixed guilds within the Cologne textile trade contained, primarily, regulations on the quality of the manufactured goods destined for export. Thus article 1 of the Cologne yarn-makers' charter, dated 14 April 1397, states: 'Whosoever, woman or maiden, wishes to learn the yarn trade in Cologne, should serve four years and no less, so that she learns to make and prepare export goods'. According to article 3, on completion of the apprentice period, 'the women who have been sworn in should check her work to establish whether it is worthy of export or not'. For the same reason the charters of the silk makers contained numerous regulations on permissible raw materials. The use of twisted silk or silk dyed with woad was forbidden. Silk cord was to be made only from brocade silk or good silk thread. No one could be permitted to fraudulently mix dyed or undyed yarn with the brocade or thread. The goldsmiths or beaters, male and female, had to ensure that they worked with good-quality precious metal.

A very different picture from that of Cologne and the other towns and regions considered so far is presented by the Italian towns of Florence, Siena, and Perugia in the fourteenth and fifteenth centuries. Here the social position of professional women engaged in goods production was not consolidated and reflected in the guild structure. Against a background of a strong early capitalist development in the main textile centres, the character of the guilds had gone through a fundamental change. They served to bolster the political-economic interests of early capitalist entrepreneurs and the town oligarchies. Under these conditions the women employed in the textile trades were doomed to remain at the level of journeymen, unskilled auxiliary staff, or, to a greater or lesser degree, wage labour. Their position was especially disadvantageous due to the abundant supply of rural labour for early capitalist enterprises.

Although the combined individual branches of the textile trade made up the sector with the most intensive export links within town goods production until the late Middle Ages, it would be wrong to assume that this was the sole area where women were employed professionally and wherein particular skilled female labour could be found.

∗ Some of the grocery trades were often practised independently by women: baking, with all its specialisations (cakes, unleavened bread, pastries); the butcher's trade; river and lake fishing; oil pressing; market gardening; and beer brewing. We know, for example, that there were female bakers in Constance, Basle, Troyes, Regensburg, Cologne, Hildesheim, Hanover, Frankfurt on Main, Görlitz, Striegau, and Halberstadt. Some idea of their importance to the supply of a large city is conveyed by the register of deaths in the Nuremberg St. Sebald parish, according to which 27 female bakers died within a period of 79 years—between 1439 and 1517. Of these, however, only 8 died between 1439 and 1477, although Nuremberg was particularly badly hit by the plague and the female mortality rate in the St. Sebald parish peaked in 1448 (at 48.6 percent) and 1449 (52.4 percent). The relative increase for the period 1477 to 1517 suggests that there was a large increase in female employment in baking in the late fifteenth century. A regulation concerning bakers and millers in Neumarkt (Silesia) toward the end of the fifteenth century decrees that baking bread, bread transportation and selling should only be practised by those men and women who had learned the trade properly from a skilled master. Female millers existed in Strasbourg, Nuremberg, Görlitz, Baden, Hildesheim, Brunswick, and Mühlhausen. One can, however, not prove if they ran the business independently. We shall ignore here the large number of women who acquired parts of mills in the form of life annuities.

Independent female master butchers are less common. In Frankfurt on Main they could only practise if they were widows and ran their dead husband's business with the help of a journeyman. The 1397 charter of the Cologne butchers granted men and women an equal position in the guild as long as they had Cologne citizenship. The Leipzig town council passed a regulation on butchers seventy years later. It allowed not only the widows of butchers but other women familiar with the trade to be active in the guild, without any restrictions. This was connected with the abolition of an extremely old custom—a sort of unwritten guild law that had until then been strictly observed—whereby journeymen and servants were not allowed to cut up or distribute meat for retail trade, even when the master was present. Because this was a trade that required a certain amount of physical strength, it had been impossible before this new regulation for widows or other independent tradeswomen to practise in Leipzig, and probably elsewhere as well. The considerable increase in the number of female butchers in Nuremberg between the years 1479 and 1517 points to a similar waiving of unwritten guild rules. There are records of fisherwomen in Nuremberg, Frankfurt on Main, Görlitz, Warsaw, and Plau (Mecklenburg). They, like their butcher counterparts, were dependent to a large degree on the labour of their sons and servants, for the catching of the fish and sometimes the selling of it, since strict market regulations excluded women from trading in fish. Yet in those places where fishing and fish processing were important for export, as for example Scania, female labour was indispensable.

Market gardening only became a trade in its own right in the more heavily populated medieval towns, since in the medium- and small-sized towns the people were still self-sufficient in garden produce and could sell what they did not need at the market. Nuremberg, Strasbourg, Hamburg, Lübeck, Danzig, and Ulm each had a population of over 20,000 in the fifteenth century and thus counted among the most densely populated medieval towns. The two towns first mentioned had gardeners' guilds. Between 1446 and 1453, 6 women in Strasbourg acquired the right of citizenship in order to be admitted to this guild—a number never surpassed by any other guild in Strasbourg. In the same period, a total of 14 women were admitted to 12 other guilds. In the tailors' guild only 2 new women members were admitted. The St. Sebald (Nuremberg) parish death register lists five female gardeners for the period 1439 to 1477.

The trade most commonly practised by women in western and central Europe apart from textile work was beer production. This seems to have thrived in every type of town, from mining settlements to maritime or export-manufacturing towns. Women were strongly represented in this trade because of the traditional division of labour between husband and wife, whereby all work done in the house was performed by the latter. It was essential that the female citizen be firmly established as a house- and landowner, since brewing rights were linked to house and property rights. Since the town council and the houseowner could not always agree on whether a house had brewing rights, the councils began to have lists drawn up by the town clerk of all the approved brewing places. This was also the basis upon which the town council demanded the brewing fee, which represented a by no means insignificant part of its income from taxes. In the annual accounts of the town budget of the Thuringian town of Mühlhausen there are, at the beginning of the fifteenth century, entries for a whole series of female citizens, many of them widows, paying such fees. Some wills testify to the value of income from brewing in making provision for widowed women. Thus we have two wills from Stralsund for the year 1347 which, before listing all the other legacies left to the wives, state that the brewing apparatus (the brewing or malt house with the brewing vessel, or just the brewing vessel and vat) should not be shared with anyone, not even with the children. The significance of brewing right for town families and unmarried women is underlined by the fact that female members of the town community joined in a conflict over the right to brew beer and to serve wine that took place in Jena in 1404 between the patrician upper stratum and the town burghers.

Records for the Saxon textile and mining town of Zwickau for the period 1503 to 1521 show that 24 women held brewing rights; some made full use of them and had a lad to help them. Among those were women by the names of the Vilberin, the Bernwalderin, the Herselmüllerin, and the Ceyslerin. Six of the 24 women are listed over the whole period among the Zwickau brewers. Of these, 3 held the malt award, the mark of quality that brewers who dealt in wholesale trade had to have branded on their beer barrels. The above-mentioned death register of the St. Sebald parish in Nuremberg mentions a number of brewers, just slightly fewer than the number of female bakers. Of the 22 female brewers buried, 17 are entered for the second period of 1479 to 1517. The Hanseatic city of Hamburg had a beer-brewing trade geared to export and likewise incorporated a considerable number of professionally independent women.

A sign of the status resulting from the particular quality of the beer produced by individual female brewers can be seen in a contract drawn up on 10 October 1420 between the town of Cologne and Fygin von Broikhusen and her husband, who was obviously present as her legal guardian. With this contract Fygin commits herself to teach two Cologne brewers how to produce *grut*[17]:

'Thus that I, the aforementioned Fygin with the knowledge, approval and permission of my aforementioned husband have agreed with the honourable wise gentlemen mayors and town council of Cologne . . . that I shall loyally and industriously and to the best of my ability teach two men to make good *grut*. These two men shall be appointed by them. They have appointed a man by the name of Hermann von Aiche, the brewer upstream near Airsbuch, whom I have already begun to teach and whom I shall continue to teach and another, whom they still have to appoint . . . without dishonestly withholding any of my knowledge of making the aforementioned *grut*. With this document I have obliged and committed myself to do this for the aforementioned gentlemen and the town of Cologne for eight consecutive years, beginning with the date of this document. And whenever they let me know that they need me for their *grut* making I shall, unless I am ill, come to their town of Cologne to instruct and teach. And for every day that I leave my house and live in Cologne for this reason they shall give me one mark of the Cologne currency to cover my labour and my upkeep'.[18] Further on, a fee of 115 Rhine guilders is mentioned, to be paid by the Cologne council by way of remuneration for Fygin's efforts. The husband vouches for his wife's reliability in honouring the contract. He states that he is prepared to offer himself as a hostage if necessary, and, as such to lodge himself, one manservant, and two horses at his own expense in one of Cologne's 'respectable inns'. The Cologne council's partners in this contract were obviously not town citizens. It is possible that they were country nobility who had fallen onto bad times—which shows up the close connection between the town and the surrounding countryside, and the fact that women from the country would sometimes come to town to make their living.

Brewing was not a guild trade everywhere. However, it always took on guild status when it moved from local trade to export business, as was the case in Lübeck, Lüneburg, Göttingen, and Magdeburg. Like the women in the textile and grocery trades, the female members of the brewing guilds could occupy various positions. For example, women by the names of de Heenyngesche and de Radesche were masters in Lüneburg; in Göttingen women employed as auxiliary helpers to carry the vats got 'nothing apart from eight pfennigs and their keep for one course of brewing'.

* One quite often comes across references to female labour in the physically more demanding professions. Of course, women worked in such service trades as laundering and bleaching, but they were also employed in trades usually practised by men—the various specialised trades within metal processing; barrel and crate making; building; and dispatch. We could add to this list rope making, soap boiling and candle making, basket making, broom and brush making, wooden and earthenware dish production, bookbinding, and doll painting.

Women were employed in metal processing if there was a thriving export trade. In Germany this was the case in Cologne, Nuremberg, and Frankfurt on Main. The St. Sebald parish in Nuremberg registers, between 1439 and 1477, 9 female coppersmiths, 7 brass mounters, 1 cutler, 1 thimble maker, 1 wiredrawer, 3 tinsmiths, 1 compass maker, and 6 pewterers. A Nuremberg town council resolution of 1535 informs us that women were commonly employed as cutlers until the early sixteenth century. As early as 1349, a council decree refers to the labour of masters' wives and daughters in the glove-making and pressing trades. Here there is explicit reference to 'any work done with a hammer', which only these women are permitted to do. In Cologne in the fifteenth century it was common for women to work as auxiliary helpers in the harness- or breast-plate-making trades. The Nuremberg thimble makers gave masters permission in 1535 to employ women but only as piece workers—that is, they were to be paid for each piece of finished work. At about the same time, guild members among the Nuremberg needle

makers were granted permission to train their offspring, both male and female, in their trade. This was also the case in Lübeck. Provided women could prove that they were born within wedlock and had an untarnished reputation they were admitted to the guild as early as 1356. Fairly liberal rules governed the use of female labour among the Cologne needle makers. They took on young men and women as apprentices and did not insist, as most other guilds did, on evidence that they were of legitimate birth. This was, however, only the case at apprenticeship level; the rules on admittance of female masters were different. Other branches of metal processing in Cologne, such as the copper mounters and pewterers, granted 'widows' rights' and allowed widows to continue the work of their husbands' workshop with the help of male employees. The copper mounters allowed the master's daughter to continue the business on his death. The guild charters of the smiths and sword makers suggest that they neither granted 'widows' rights' nor allowed women to be employed in the trade. By way of contradiction, however, we find that three female smiths—of whom one at least, Fya upper Bach, the 'smithy of Siberg', seems to have been an independent master—held office in 1389 and 1417. When she was granted Cologne citizenship from 1389 to 1398, she was already entered as a smith. We also have evidence of 'widows' rights' in the sword-maker trade at the end of the fifteenth century. In Frankfurt on Main in the fourteenth and fifteenth centuries there were women working as metal casters, cutlers, bolt makers, scythe smiths, sieve makers, and knife grinders; in Augsburg they were active among the wheel makers, cutlers, blacksmiths, and locksmiths. Even a modest central German town such as Grimma had a regulation concerning male and female masters of smiths' shops in the middle of the fifteenth century, designed in particular to regulate the mutual poaching of apprentices and servants. According to a 1492 ruling on masters and journeymen in the small hammersmith workshops of St. Gallen in Switzerland, women were admitted to the trade, participated as equal members at the annual general meetings, and had an equal say in economic decisions.

If we take the pronounced division of labour within the house of the craftsman into account, it can be assumed that by no means could all these economically independent female craftworkers spend their work days in the workshop. A female master or the wife of a master must have been in a position to evaluate the quality of the work and to provide facilities in which careful and profitable work could be carried out. Moreover, they had to oversee the sale of the wares produced in the workshop.

In towns that lay on trading routes and in the large sea-trading towns, the most important professions, apart from the grocery and textile ones, were those related to trading—crate making, strap and wheel making, rope making, coopery, and dispatch. These required significant manpower and provided another source of employment for economically independent women. Thus, for example, the ruling on the Lübeck crate makers of 1508 permits old and ailing widows to carry on their husband's trade with the help of a male journeyman until their own death. The council charges them only one-third of the guild membership fee. These widows were allowed to continue employing an apprentice. If there was a son, the widow was supposed to work with him until he was of age and could do the work independently. 'Widows' rights' were still valid in the Lübeck wheel-makers' guild until the beginning of the sixteenth century, although they only applied to women who were no longer of an age when they were likely to remarry. In the mid- to late fifteenth century there was a female member of the Strasbourg cartwrights' guild. The rope-maker trade was practised by female citizens of Frankfurt on Main, Nuremberg, Leipzig, and Erfurt. In 1425 the Erfurt council negotiated a contract between rope makers and beaker makers according to which the wives of the latter could produce hoisting ropes and sell them elsewhere. Source material relating to the transport and dispatch trades refers to female wool packers

working in England in 1507. These women were based in Southampton and had formed an organisation similar to that of a guild that was run by two chairpersons elected annually from their own ranks. In Frankfurt on Main, female cart loaders were represented in the transport trades. Both of these packing and loading trades undoubtedly required a lot of physical strength; this is underlined by a source relating to the wool packers which states that 'they lifted the bales and sacks with their own hands'.

Without attempting to give an exhaustive list of the guild trades practised by women, it is worth giving brief mention to the women members of the guilds in the building trade, who come up fairly frequently in the source material. A 1271 ruling on the masons, plasterers, carpenters, coopers, cartwrights, winnowers, and wood turners of Basle allows women to join the guild as long as their husbands are still alive, and providing that they remain widows should their husbands die. This ruling can hardly refer to women doing professional work in the trade. It is more likely to refer to those who joined the guild but had only co-operative and social duties. This was, however, no longer the case in the building and building-related trades in the late Middle Ages. Written and pictorial sources suggest that women were employed in the hard physical work involved in the building, mortar-mixing, roof-making, and glazier trades. In Frankfurt on Main there were female claywall makers and women employed in the lime works; in Nuremberg there were female glaziers. In Mühlhausen (Thuringia) there is a record of a woman clay transporter in the fifteenth century and a maid who was injured by a servant while lifting clay from a pit. In 1437 this woman demanded compensation and repayment of the medical costs; she was represented in court by her brother. In Strasbourg from 1452 to 1453, two women joined the masons' guild and were simultaneously granted the right to town citizenship. Women were employed in the ore works in mining towns, and although we only have pictorial sources as evidence for this, they state the case quite eloquently. Thus Hans Hesse, for example, depicts on the reverse side of the Annaberg mine altar a female worker, in one scene hard at work and in another dressed in holiday clothing. Another, somewhat earlier pictorial representation of a female worker at the ore mines comes from Kuttenberg in Bohemia and dates from the fifteenth century. Pictorial sources from the middle of the following century, such as the illustrations for the works of Georgius Agricola *(De re metallica, On Mining)*, show women sorters at silver mines.

✳ Before we go on to look at the female professions not directly connected with the trade and the craft life of the town, it is worth reflecting for a moment on the effect that guild membership had on the status and position of the female craftworker in the town community. Here we first have to make the distinction between full membership and part membership. The former concerns the economically independent craftworker, who would usually be independently entitled to town citizenship but would have to apply for it if she were a stranger to the town. As with members of the purely female guilds in Paris, Cologne, and Zurich, full membership was conditional on completion of a guild-approved apprenticeship training. Part membership was particularly common amongst widows, who on account of 'widows' rights' were tolerated in the guilds. In England, a man's right to town citizenship could be passed on to his widow. The fact that numerous guild rulings on the 'widows' rights' state that she must have a competent journeyman in order to carry on her husband's profession would suggest that professional experience could not always be taken for granted.

Finally, another form of female membership existed and was probably the most common—a joint membership that included the wives of the male guild members and both expressed the fraternal-religious aspect of the guilds and acknowledged the role played by the wives in all the town trades. This included supervision and care of the maids, journeymen, and apprentices who were part of the master's household and provided competent back-up in the workshop.

Full membership meant for the economically independent female craftworker that she had to fulfill the same duties as her male colleagues. This involved, in the first place, meeting the usual terms of admittance, such as producing a birth certificate that proved that she was born in wedlock and testified to her untarnished reputation and, of course, payment of the membership fee. Daughters of local masters were usually entitled to a 50-percent reduction of the fee and exempted from having to produce a birth certificate. (In the fifteenth century, women who were strangers to the guild sometimes had to prove that not only they but their parents and grandparents were of good repute.) The economically independent female craftworker had to perform the duties that were required to varying extents by the different guilds. She had to contribute to the guard and defence duties of the guild members, not in person but through her financial contributions. Defence duty was regulated in such a way that one had to equip a representative, either by oneself or with other women, or keep a horse, again by oneself or with others. Details on the horse and pieces of armoury that had to be supplied are available for the Strasbourg clothmakers' and weavers' guild and for the citizens of the towns of Mühlhausen (Thuringia) and Görlitz. In some towns, women had not only the right but also the obligation to take part in the guild meetings. Thus article 12 of the Hamburg linen-weavers' decree of 1375 states that men or women who fail to attend the guild meeting are liable to a fine of six pfennigs and ten shillings, unless their absence is due to illness. If they failed to appear at the meetings more than three times they could be deprived of their title of master for one year. An updating of the bakers' statute in Striegau (Silesia) dating from 1393 likewise lists a penalty for the failure of men and women to attend guild meetings. Female masters of the yarn-drawer trade in this town were also present at guild meetings.

Widows were admitted to a large number of guilds and granted membership for a limited period or for life. These craftworkers, who produced their wares alone or with a son who was still under-age (an apprentice boy or a journeyman), were presumably also subject to the above-mentioned duties for economically independent female masters. A greater degree of security and more recognition was guaranteed, of course, by the master title, achievement of which was based on the successful completion of a recognized period of learning—which could be accomplished, for example, by apprenticing oneself to one's husband or father: the Neuss linen weavers, for example, decided in 1461, when trade was prospering, to allow themselves to take on their wives and children as apprentices.

The third type of guild membership stems from the co-operative nature of the guilds, which is reflected in the duty to support elderly and invalid members or relatives of members, and also in the communal celebration of a religious ceremony. Funeral attendance was, in particular, mandatory for guild members. Although the activity of the master's wife tended to be limited to this religious/co-operative side of guild life, it still served to enrich the lives of many female citizens, giving them the opportunity to leave their own four walls. The responsibility of the master's wife for all matters concerning the house and the workshop of the master was recognized by, for example, the Zurich town council when, in 1429, it obliged masters who could not attend meetings in person to send their wives as their representatives.

The number of economically independent females who on completion of an apprenticeship or by virtue of 'widows' rights' could practise a profession was, in the larger central European towns and in a considerable number of the medium-sized trading and manufacturing towns, quite significant. The reasons for this are varied, but all derive more or less from the economic make-up of the town economies in the late Middle Ages—a significant feature of which was the poverty suffered by craft families who begat more children than they could

afford to support. Thus several women and one wool weaver, Jörg Bermenter, submitted the following written plea to the town council of Heilbronn in 1509: 'If now one of us or one of our husbands falls ill, it is obvious that we all of us are needy and poor people, among whom many have not received three farthings and some none at all from their parents, so that we have to keep ourselves through our own strenuous labour. And if it be forbidden for us to do the work we have done since childhood, then we will have to resort to begging in order to feed our children as well as the sick husband'.[19] Such poverty is underlined by the phenomenon of child labour, not only in yarn preparation and spinning, work for which even four- to five-year-old children were employed, but for work as shepherds and as cheap labour for domestic help and in vineyards.

The increase in the number of women working independently of their husbands was due, too, to the often sizable gaps in the labour supply brought about by high mortality rates in the towns as a result of the plague, overwork, and malnutrition. Male mortality rates seem not to be higher than the female ones and are sometimes even lower. The victims among the male population probably included independent masters, or journeymen who had completed their apprenticeships. The gaps that their deaths left in the labour force were filled not only by the widows of masters but by circumspect women whose husbands had different professions. Another fact to bear in mind is that the flow of women from the agricultural population to the towns continued unabated throughout the Middle Ages.

A certain, although perhaps only secondary, influence might have been exercised by the instability of the marriage bonds/vows, which we will come back to later. It was not uncommon for men to live in bigamy and for married couples to live and work separated by the town walls.

If we want to cover the position of women within the guild crafts, we cannot ignore those women whose work was most common and who, moreover, provided a back-up for the rest of the professional structure of the medieval town. These were the female domestic staff, who had no set professional status and whose duties covered a wide range of tasks, which included providing auxiliary labour in the workshop. Numerous sources also describe them as performing the tasks of female journeymen or wage labour.

A recent examination of the classification of the female population in the social structure of the medieval trading and manufacturing town of Trier, carried out on the basis of the tax registers of 1364 and their topographical breakdown, has shown that women are most highly represented, at 51 percent, in the lower economic strata. In certain districts of the town, near charitable or religious establishments and in the weaver districts, women represent 70 or even 100 percent of the population in the lower strata. Obviously we are dealing here primarily with female workers in the weaver trade. Likewise in Basle in 1454 and Frankfurt on Main in 1495, the proportion of women in the lowest tax category is relatively high. In Basle 69.5 percent of this category (covering 1,072 people) in possession of 1 to 30 guilders are women and 45 percent are men; in Frankfurt on Main, out of 979 people liable for tax and in possession of up to 20 guilders 61.9 percent are female and 35.3 percent male. On the other hand, three districts of the town of Augsburg have records of an almost equal number of servant lads and maids. They record 334 servant lads (including 25 merchants' manservants) as opposed to 339 maids.

Results of available socio-statistical surveys indicate that overseas and overland trading towns in the late Middle Ages with a relatively broad upper stratum of long-distance and wholesale traders and scholars had a relatively large number of maids, whereas manufacturing towns had a larger proportion of servant lads.[20] There are clear indications that different wages were paid female and male domestic staff in professions such as wine making or construction. Thus female workers in the vineyards of Mühlhausen (Thuringia) were paid half

a man's (i.e., a child's) wage. Even under such pay conditions, female employment rates were high. On Würzburg building sites, for example, a large amount of female labour was employed on a daily basis between 1428 and 1524. The low-skill labourers received the following average wage, reckoned in pfennigs:

Year	Number of female workers	Wage	Number of male workers	Wage
1428 to 1449	323	7.7	13	11.6
1450 to 1474	1472	9.0	381	12.6
1475 to 1499	209	8.3	131	11.2
1500 to 1524	429	9.2	237	12.7

The pay conditions in the Würzburg building trade were no exception. This can be seen in a decree on maximum prices and wages issued to all towns and markets in the Steiermark, according to which serving lads, who carried stones or mortar, were paid 8 pfennigs per day and women doing similar work were to be paid only 7 pfennigs. A similar disparity in the wages paid to male and female workers is seen in the calculation of the average weekly and annual wage for two church parishes in Basle for the year 1451. The average weekly wage has been calculated for 123 maids and 157 (male) journeymen, and comes to 20.3 pfennigs for the former and 38.7 for the latter. The average annual pay for maids was 3.8 Rhine gold guilders and for serving lads 7.3. The pay for maids who had completed an apprenticeship and were actually female journeymen was better. Thus, for example, the female haircloth makers in Mühlhausen were paid the same piece-wage as the men. The real domestic maids were also at a disadvantage because part of their wage was kept back to buy them clothing (coats, shoes, skirts) or bed-linen and was only paid at the employers' discretion or after a legal complaint had been lodged.

In an earlier period, the Franciscan friar Bertold von Regensburg (1220–1272) had attacked in his preaching those who deprive 'working people of their well-earned wage' and who lend usurer's money instead of remunerating work done. The situation in the fourteenth and fifteenth centuries had certainly not changed for the better.

✳ Let us now turn to those professions not directly connected with the crafts or merchant trading, or tangential to them. In the overseas and overland trading towns, large manufacturing centres, and medium-sized and smaller towns situated close to important trading routes, the tavern- and innkeeper was indispensable to commerce; she could arrange cash loans or credit, and often helped store and organise the transportation of goods. An inn of good repute offered accommodation for long periods of time and had spacious storerooms and stables. Well-known inns served as meeting places for business and trade partners during trade fairs and markets; a tale by Ruprecht von Würzburg, written around 1300, tells of the rich Verdun merchant Bertram, who came to a well-known inn in Provins. When Bertram has finished his meal, so reports Ruprecht, the innkeeper insists on gossiping about wives and the merchant ends up having to prove his wife's loyalty by engaging in a wager.

The running of inns and taverns certainly required the help and co-operation of the innkeeper's wife. If she fell ill or died, her absence was felt by the guest as much as by the husband. One guest's regret is expressed in a letter from Martin Behaim, dated 17 September 1455, to his brother Lienhart, in which he announces the death of a lady innkeeper in Salzburg by the name of Turm-eckerin.

Members of the ruling patricians' town council met in the inns attached to the town houses, and citizens would go there to seek information on town affairs. Likewise, taprooms and ale-houses were designed to meet social and information needs—both of through-travellers and of local inhabitants.

Particular discretion was required of innkeepers. One very plucky woman of Erfurt, Katharina Johans, who dared to write letters badgering a well-known customer

into paying his drinking debts, had to make a public apology for her behaviour at a council meeting. The incident was recorded in the town records, since it was a matter of upholding the honour and good name of a citizen.

The successful female tavern-keepers with large hostelries had to be well versed in many aspects of life. They not only had to cater to the physical well-being of their

Husband and wife carry a large stone which will complete the roof of a chapel.
Woodcut, printed by Peter Drach, Speyer, early sixteenth century. In: Albert Schramm, *Der Bilderschmuck der Frühdrucke.* Vol. XVI. Leipzig, 1933, ill. 450.

guests but were expected to provide entertainment for them. They would gather information on the currency exchange rates and political events and pass these on; and they arranged credit, acted as pawn-brokers, and mediated in commercial transactions. In a letter dated 24 October 1417, one guest does not hesitate to approach Zwickau innkeeper Dorothea Storchin (later the wife

A female distiller.
Woodcut, printed by Johann Zainer, Augsburg, 1498. In: Albert Schramm, *Der Bilderschmuck der Frühdrucke.* Vol. V. Leipzig, 1922, ill. 452.

of Bastian 'aus der Müntze') as a 'respectable wise woman' in order to arrange credit. The diverse activities of the female innkeeper can be seen even more clearly in the reports of the most frequently mentioned Görlitz innkeeper, a lady by the name of Bleckerynne. She put up the guests who came for the woad trade, as well as guests of the town council, church officials, and, in emergencies, even the town mercenaries. Another large tavern was run by Orthey Rorerynne, who on several occasions received payments from the town council to cover the expenses of servants of the crown and who could, when necessary, put up fifty mercenaries with fifty horses. Another woman called 'old Rychterin' is recorded as possessing farmsteads and lodging woad transporters and mercenaries.

In contrast to the prosperous female innkeepers, the woman who had only a taproom/ale-house often had to cope without the help of a serving boy or girl; the Marseilles town council, for one, decreed in the thirteenth century that only the owner or the owner's spouse could serve beer or wine. There were other problems as well, such as conflicts between taproom owners and those citizens who had brewing rights, since the latter would serve the ever-popular ale in their own houses.

Women who ran the modest taverns and inns sometimes tried to supplement their income by treating minor ailments. Johannes Butzbach, recalling his travels in the 1490s, tells of a Nuremberg innkeeper who could fully heal his feet, which caused him great pain. He also attributes his timely homecoming to the intelligence of a Bohemian innkeeper in Karlsbad, one of whose spa guests—a Nuremberg merchant taking the waters with his family whom the innkeeper gave detailed information on Butzbach's financial straits—agreed to take Butzbach to Nuremberg in his carriage. A very different picture of the female innkeeper is painted by the Englishman John Gower (ca. 1330–1400)—a friend of Geoffrey Chaucer (ca. 1343–1400)—in his *Mirour de l'Omme.* He characterises an equally enterprising woman as follows: 'But to say the truth in this instance the trade of regratery belongeth by right the rather to women. But if a woman be at it she in her stinginess useth much more machination and deceit than a man; for never alloweth she the profit on a single crumb to escape her, nor faileth to hold her neighbour to paying his price. All who beseech her do but lose their time, for nothing doth she by courtesy, as anyone who drinketh in her house knoweth full well'.[21]

∗ Social work and medical services—apart from in the English towns with a relatively small number of nuns and female religious bodies—was performed by establishments such as convents and Beguine houses, and by women outside the religious orders—doctors, midwives, their helpers and apprentices, bathkeepers, and others, especially those familiar with folk medicine. Both groups were indispensable until men began to be given medical training at universities, and consequently formed a professional body of doctors with a sound theoretical knowledge. Women were excluded from this new professional body, the one exception being a certain Francisca, wife of Mattheus Romano, who was granted recognition and approval as a surgeon with university training by the Duke of Calabria, Charles. The fourteenth and fifteenth centuries seem to be a transition period during which women's gradual squeezing out of health care only just began.

It was in Paris, one of the university centres of western Europe, where the medical faculty, deaf to all criticism, was particularly vigorous in its attempts to ban females from the medical profession. Here the thirty-year-old Jacqueline Felicie de Alemania was accused as early as 1322 of not respecting the ban which forbade anyone not in possession of a faculty decree and the approval of the Sorbonne rector from practising in Paris and the surrounding area. This ban also affected a Jewish woman, Johanna Belota, as well as Margarete von Ypernn, both of whom were well-known surgeons. In Germany a number of female doctors did enjoy the recognition of the town councils. In 1394, for example,

Religious upbringing meant that a doctor could be called only when women of good repute were present.
Miniature from *Chirurgia*, by Gerard of Cremona, twelfth century, Codex Series Nova 2641, fol. 60 r. Österreichische Nationalbibliothek, Vienna

the daughter of a since-deceased town doctor in Frankfurt on Main twice received remuneration from the town council for the healing of wounded soldiers. A medieval female army surgeon is also recorded in the Swiss *Spiezer Bilder-Chronik* (Spiez pictorial chronicle) of Diebold Schilling. In the fifteenth century, sixteen female doctors are mentioned in Frankfurt on Main, but their actual number is unknown. Most frequent mention is given to Jewish doctors and opticians. In 1457 the council refused a female Jewish doctor the right to stay in the town. On the other hand, in 1492, 1494, 1496, and

A midwife and an assistant stand by at the birth of twins (fol. 41 v.).

A midwife supervises the afterbirth (fol. 43 r.).
Miniatures from *Chirurgia,* by Gerard of Cremona, twelfth century, Codex Series Nova 2641. Österreichische Nationalbibliothek, Vienna

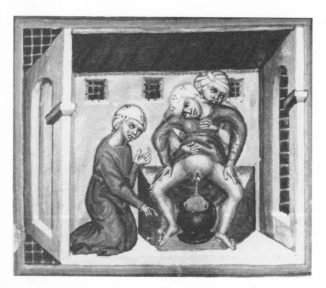

1499 the council allowed one, apparently very popular, female Jewish doctor to stay in the town without demanding the payment usually required from Jewish strangers for overnight stays. The female doctor's request to be allowed to live outside the Jewish quarter was, however, refused. In 1494 another ban was imposed on a Jewish female doctor. One female doctor and a married couple, both of whom were doctors, had practices in Hildesheim in the late fifteenth century. In 1477 a woman with medical knowledge received payment for looking after the wounded. The Görlitz town council's accounts record the employment of another woman, Tauwaldynne, for the healing of the town clerk's infirmities. According to Hermann Weinsberg, one woman was regularly consulted on medical matters in Cologne until the mid-sixteenth century.

We have plenty of examples, but it remains impossible to establish the extent to which these female 'doctors', with no formal medical training, could draw on medical knowledge to treat the various ailments.

One area of medicine where women's contribution was indispensable throughout the Middle Ages was in the treatment of female ailments. While the Catholic church forbade doctors to do practical examinations of women, and the women themselves were often too shy to go to a doctor, women would turn to a member of their own sex.

The midwife tended to be the great authority on female health care. Obviously she could draw on her practical experience, which from a very early date had been coupled with the theoretical knowledge of the doctor. The early miniatures in Gerard of Cremona's (ca. 1114–1187) *Chirurgia* show birth scenes, which confirms that this was the case.[22] The famous medieval work on female health care, the *Liber Trotula,* the origin of which is still unknown, leads us to surmise that there was a connection between the doctor and the female folk doctor, or the midwife.

It seems that such co-operation was common in Flanders, where it was not unusual for doctor and midwife

A woman is treated simultaneously with a herbal bath and herbal drink.
From *Liber Trotula*, 1446/66, Hs. 593, fol. 15 v. Municipal Library, Bruges

Women assist in the treatment of a patient laid out on an extension bed. Miniature from *Chirurgia*, by Gerard of Cremona, twelfth century, Codex Series Nova 2641, fol. 76 v. Österreichische Nationalbibliothek, Vienna

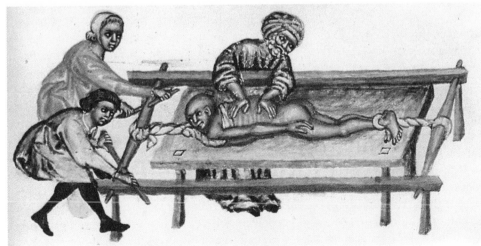

to be married. This is known to have been the case in Mons and Ghent. In the fifteenth century a Latin and a local dialect version of the *Liber Trotula* appeared in Flanders.

An English dialect version of the work is known to have existed in the fourteenth century. The author, in his introduction to the translation, makes the educational purpose clear: 'As women of our own tongue do better read and understand this language than any other, and every woman lettered read it to other unlettered and help them and counsel them in their maladies withouten showing their disease to man, I have this drawn and written in English'.[23]

The efforts of doctors and midwives to improve the health awareness and medical care of the female population were supported in numerous central European towns by the town councils. They employed town doctors and tried to lighten the load of the midwives.

The latter were not obliged to pay town taxes or perform guard duties, they were supplied with firewood, and in some towns the midwife's husband was excused from guard duty. The births on the whole took place at home. Those who gave birth in hospital did so through chance. This explains the minimal capacity in the Paris maternity home *(office d'accouchées)*, which in the fifteenth century had twenty-four beds, with two to three women with babies per bed. In some large towns the midwives employed by the town council were given a regular wage. In 1381 the town of Nuremberg guaranteed them 1 guilder every three months. In Bruges their wage was calculated at 12 groschen per day provided that they worked 270 days per year. In other towns the midwives had to fight longer for a guaranteed regular income and lived from the voluntary payments made by grateful fathers or from gifts. This had the unfortunate consequence that some midwives neglected the women from the lower social stratum of the town. There is evidence of this in the Ulm decree on midwives dating from 1491 and the Nördlingen decree of 1517. These strictly forbid any union of midwives, since such unions could

Women place cupping glasses.
Miniature from *Chirurgia*, by Gerard of Cremona, twelfth century, Codex Series Nova 2641, fol. 62 v. Österreichische Nationalbibliothek, Vienna

hurt the common folk. The decrees guaranteed the town council more influence over the methods used by the midwives and were an attempt to ensure that the townswomen could be guaranteed competent help during delivery. Midwives were required to sit an entrance exam before the town council and experienced women of the town. The apprentice midwives and the helpers present at the birth were guaranteed a gift of money from the new mother's family which the midwife was forbidden to 'pocket'. The regulations also covered the careful training of the helpers, who were not to be prevented from performing their duties by work in the midwife's house.

The town council also used the midwives as a form of social control and demanded reports from them of any lapses in the moral standards of the town. Such midwife decrees came into force in Regensburg in 1452, in Heilbronn in the fifteenth century, and in Constance in 1525. A number of other towns required that midwives swear on oath that they would perform those duties listed by the town. This was the case in Colmar in the fifteenth century and Würzburg in 1480.

The social tasks of the town citizens also included the care of foundlings and young orphans, either in their own houses or in homes established for the purpose. The records of the Ulm orphan and foundling home give us some idea of the importance of this work. In the fifteenth century it housed on average 120 to 150 children per year. According to a decree of 1491 only those children could be admitted whose parents had been resident in the town for 10 years; in 1503 this period was extended to 20 years. The women of the town would also help in the care of the elderly and sick, in the running of hospitals and in the organisation of funerals.

The picture of late medieval town life, especially in the large and medium-sized towns, would remain incomplete if we failed to mention the attempts of female citizens to make their way into the intellectual-artistic professions. Such attempts were usually in line with the specific interests of their families, since contributions by the wife and children to the husband's profession were not limited to trade and craftwork. Women helped with book illumination, scribe and teaching work, and the running of town offices. This meant, however, that the women and girls had to have a certain degree of education. This was usually provided by private tutors, in particular by church scholars without benefice, but in some cases the parents themselves would devote time to their daughters' upbringing and education. Beguine houses and convents also had a share in offering young girls a general education.

✷ The development of the secular schools undoubtedly had a favourable influence on the provision of education for the young girls of the towns. At the end of the thirteenth century, educational establishments in Flanders and Paris allowed the daughters of the upper social stratum to receive outside the parental home the elementary education in reading, writing, and arithmetic that was becoming increasingly necessary. Thus the future abbess of the Cistercian convent Nazareth, a patrician's daughter by the name of Beatrijs van Tienen, had been sent to school at the age of seven to learn the 'free arts'. Before this she had been given instruction by her mother, an early thirteenth-century 'merchant woman'. Another thirteenth-century Cistercian nun in Flanders, Ida Lewenis (b. 1260), was educated in a secular school that taught children of both sexes. In 1320 Duke John of Lorraine gave permission for five schools to be opened in Brussels to give girl pupils a basic education. Brussels actually already had, apart from the boys' school, one primary school for girls, which, however, gave instruction in the mother tongue only. Paris at the end of the thirteenth century had twenty-one female school teachers who acted as headmistresses for such elementary girls' schools. They were under the authority of the choirmaster of Notre Dame, whose permission was required by teachers before they could give instruction. Apart from these, Paris in the fourteenth century had even lower-level mixed schools, separate schools for girls and boys being first introduced in 1357.

The fourteenth-century French crown lawyer and political publicist Pierre Dubois in his reformist pamphlet 'On Recapturing the Holy Land' (De recuperatione terrae sanctae), which reads like a medieval peace programme, gives clear confirmation of women's access to a minimum education and of a desire among those in the leading town upper stratum for a more advanced level of education. His programme includes a proposal for educational reform, and it is typical of this bourgeois reformer to include in it the education of girls. In order to ensure France's leading role over all the other major powers, in Europe, Byzantium, and the Orient, Dubois worked out a detailed plan for the education of boys and girls from the age of four or six to sixteen or eighteen years. According to his plan, 100 or more pupils, male and female, were to be installed in boarding schools (which were buildings confiscated from the Order of the Knight Templars or of the Knights of St. John of Jerusalem). The plan abolished the only elementary-level education for the girls. Like the boys, the girls had to acquire a sound knowledge of Latin and one other foreign language. The curriculum also envisaged an introductory course to the natural sciences, especially medicine and surgery, and instruction in some aspects of pharmacy.

There is little evidence of girls attending the elementary public schools in England. The author of the fourteenth-century English version of the *Liber Trotula* counts on literate English women to pass on the book's medical hints to their compatriots, which suggests that women's education here was a matter of individual endeavour. The prosperous Italian town burghers also employed private tutors for their daughters.

A large number of citizens, probably those from the middle strata of the town burghers, sent their children to the elementary schools, mainly to learn to read. (Villani in 1338 gives a figure of eight to ten thousand male and female school pupils for Florence, which gives some indication of how common provision of this level of education was.)

In Germany and Switzerland one can trace the beginnings of private and public (in the sense that the town council had some influence over them) school education back to the turn of the fourteenth and fifteenth centuries. Around 1400 the town council of Memmingen sent a certain Martin Huber to teach in a girls' school. He had to swear on oath before the town council that he would behave in a manner befitting the position and that he would not give instruction to any male pupils. There was still a strict separation of the sexes in the schools. In Emmerich the girls' school in 1445 was still formally under the aegis of the church, which had the right to enrol and dismiss the female teachers, but the town council had the right to nominate candidates for teaching

posts. It could make further nominations should the deacon and the chapter object to its original candidates. The Bamberg school decree of 1491 requires that German primary schoolteachers marry other teachers. This school decree also expressly requires that only those schoolmistresses who were really 'learned' be hired to teach children reading, writing, singing, and the general moral and ethical norms based on Catholic theology.

The traveller's diary *(Wanderbüchlein)* of Johannes Butzbach informs us that both Nuremberg and Bamberg, because of their high level of schooling, attracted pupils from other towns. Nuremberg also seems to have had numerous lower-level elementary schools toward the end of the fifteenth century. A chronicle recording the singing of the Nuremberg schoolchildren during the visit of Kaiser Frederick III tells us that male and female schoolteachers had pupils of both sexes: 'In the year 1487, German schoolmasters with their boys and girls and likewise the schoolmistresses with their boys and girls went to the Nuremberg fortress and into the chapel of the castle and sang German songs therein and afterwards they sang under the lime trees in the castle courtyard'. The Kaiser rewarded them with a sum of guilders which was afterward taken from the schoolmasters and mistresses by the Nuremberg town council, demonstrating the teaching staff's subordination to the town council. The Kaiser must have come to hear of the council's action, because he ordered all the schoolchildren to appear before him on the following Sunday. 'And thereafter, on the Sunday, about four thousand schoolchildren gathered, as ordered, below the castle walls and were given gingerbread, flat cakes, wine and beer'.[24] Even if one allows for the tendency in medieval reporting to exaggerate, it can still be assumed that Nuremberg had a large number of schoolchildren and that the chronicler took a certain pride in Nuremberg's flourishing school education.

A primary school under the authority of the town council also existed in the Saxon textile and mining town of Zwickau in the early fifteenth century. At the begin-

12 Mary, wearing a crown and portrayed as a temple virgin, works with a weaving shuttle and shaft at a loom.
Window with Mary as a temple virgin, ca. 1350/60, from Strassengel, near Graz. Österreichisches Museum für angewandte Kunst

Following pages

13 Pious members of the lay community of the Humiliates work with a pedal loom and spinning wheel.
Miniature from *Historia ordinis Humiliatorum*, ca. 1421, Codex 301 fol. 3 r. Biblioteca Ambrosiana, Milan

14 A woman uses bellows in a joiner's workshop.
Miniature from the Codex of Baltazar Behem, 1505, plate 14. University Library, Cracow

Caplm vij:

Aliq quedā matrone ex deuocione oftrū fecerūt q̄ plura cenobia re
giofar iclufic ptibz acenobijs virox pẽdaciam fepata ut fecerūt ma
rone domine foror de blafono mediolani pangmētacione ordinie Et que
obmittebāt ex erciciũ manuale p̄ fubftētacione vite fine Heo philere qui
fuit ofeiolar de vie ufq̄ ad fufeeption̄ omniū ofict et regule ene fe
burie canonicae ṗadebar ṗ iaeliit ṗdicte forores de blafono iſto
eligebāt inuifter cui obediebāt ut matrē:

15 Women also participated in hard physical work, such as washing ore in the mines.
Panel painting by Hans Hesse, 'The Ore Washer', 1521, Annaberg Altar, detail. Church of St. Anne, Annaberg-Buchholz

Following pages

16 Woman giving birth attended by a midwife and her assistant.
Incunabulum from Alexis Guillaume, *Passe-temps de toute homme*, Paris, by Antoine Verard, 1505, Vellum 2249. Bibliothèque Nationale, Paris

17 Pregnant woman undergoing treatment with coriander in order to speed up labour. The midwives are wearing round bonnets, and two assistants are in attendance.
From Pseudo-Apuleius, *De herbarium virtutibus*, *Codex Vindobonensis* 93, fol. 102 v. Österreichische Nationalbibliothek, Vienna

18 Nursing mother receives a drink from the midwife; an assistant attends to the child.
Painting by Hans Süss of Kulmbach, 'Birth of the Virgin', 1510/11. Museum der bildenden Künste, Leipzig

19 While two women attend to a corpse, alms are distributed in the background for the salvation of the dead person's soul.
Miniature from a manuscript, ca. 1430, Ms. lat. 1158, fol. 137. Bibliothèque Nationale, Paris

Car sur noz piedz ne nous tenons
Et nul lieu nallons ne venons
Et ne vsons de vertu humaine
Jusqua long temps et a grant paine

Du cry de lenfant haultement
Et des douleurs denfantement

Pur la misere de na=
ture
Demonstrer toute crea
ture
Humaine crie a sa naiss
sance
Cest de douleur vraye congnoissance

102

ri. cura eius adlumbricos.

Et coriandrum cecoque adstias in oleo in capite mittis.
mulier ut cito pariat.

Recte coriandri sem grana. xi. au. vii. et in linteolo mundo filo
de tela alligab a puer. aut puella. ligo ad sem sinistru. ppe singuine tene
at et mox ut omia partus fuit p̄actus remecha cito tollat ne intestine
equantur.

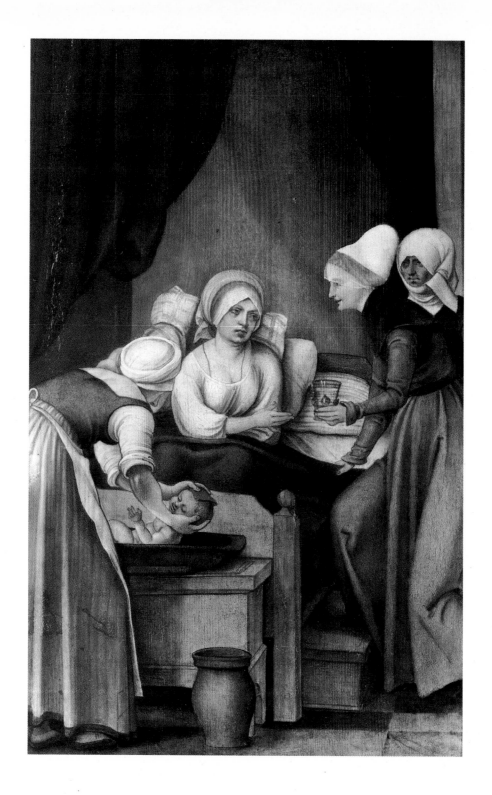

82

Sur la iiij.e Journee

parquoy Ie dy selon mon Iuggemet
que lomme qui selon dieu veult
viure ne doit pour fonge delaif
fer a faire les biens par lui pro
pofez ne faire auffi chofe quelcxe
ne mauuaife combien que les
fonges femblent eftre fauorables
abien ou a mal faire et quilz fe
blent conforter par aucuns argu
mens a nulz desquelz len ne doit

croire et ainfi par oppofite bone chofe
neft me adiouster foy a tous fonges
ains laiffons atant de fonges et
venons a compter de noe pppofi
nouuelle

Et apres fenfuit au long le copie
de la pppofr nouuelle comptee par
pamphile fur la iiij.e iournee dont
philofeurate eft for

En brefec une cité de
lombardie fu autrefoiz
ung noble homme ap
pelle fire noude pont
caruere qui entre fes autres enfans
auoit une fille nomee andriole
Iueune et affez belle et a dont
non mariee Andriole fenamou
ra dung fien voifin appelle gabriot
Iouuencel de baffe condition mais

plain de bonnes meurs bel de corps
et plaifant Andriole aladauce dung
varlet de la maifon de fon pere
fift tant que gabriot ne feut pas
feulement fon eftre ame de la fille
ains mefmement gabriot fu me
nez au foulas de chafcune fdte
par maintes fois en ung beau ver
gier qui eftoit de fire noir pere de
la fouuenelle Et afin que autre

20 Women, whose dress suggests they are Beguines, are stopped by the town guard as they carry off an apparently lifeless man.
Miniature by a Flemish master from *Androlla and Gabriel*, ca. 1440, Ms. 5070, fol. 164 v. Bibliothèque de l'Arsenal, Paris

21 The maid carrying water, to the right of the picture, serves the lovers.
Miniature from Guilbert de Metz, *Richard et Catelle*, late fourteenth century, Ms. 5070, fol. 116. Bibliothèque de l'Arsenal, Paris

Following pages

22 Cook at the stove. On the wall hangs a pair of bellows; the window has diamond-shaped panes.
Painting by the Master of the Scots Altar, 'Christ before Kaiphas', ca. 1470, detail. Benedictine Abbey of the Scots, Vienna

23 Female burghers and maids in a scene from everyday town life. The maids carry loads on their heads.
Painting by Marx Reichlich, 'The Visitation of Mary', ca. 1515, detail. Österreichische Galerie, Vienna

24 Kitchen in a town burgher's house with stove, open fire and chimney. Kitchen maid and servant are distinguished from each other by their dress. Both are bonnetless—that is, they are unmarried.
Painting by the Master of the Scots Altar, 'Birth of the Virgin', ca. 1470, detail. Benedictine Abbey of the Scots, Vienna

25 'Priests' women', concubines and housekeepers of the clerics, were taken into custody by the town in 1405. The council expected the clerics to pay good money for their release. Miniature from Diebold Schilling, *Spiezer Bilder-Chronik*, 1485, plate 239. Municipal and University Library, Berne

Do man zalt von gottes geburt/ as lxxx vo Tag warent
vil pfaffen dienen Im lande / Vñ herren die von
Beron die herren von luen getan / Do meinten die
priester man hette sis dienen nit ze straffen noch
von luen ze wisen / Do gebuten die von Beron
den pfaffen dienen allen von luen ze gan / By
einer pene / do wurden si etwas uwes von luen
vnd enelten das nit lang / Do hies man die selben
alle vachen vnd wurden in die besten geleit do
nit des zitglocken turn ist / Ze stund kamen et
lich priester vnd verburgeten die weren uß/ die aber
nit us kamen/ denen erging es als harnach stat

26 Shepherdess who—judging by her clothes—may also have been in the service of the town.
Panel painting by Giovanni Santi, 'Mary with Child Worshipped by a Shepherdess and St. Sebastian', second half of the fifteenth century, detail. Staatliches Lindenau Museum, Altenburg

27 A female sutler in the service of the Bernese army carries a halberd.
Miniature from Diebold Schilling, *Spiezer Bilder-Chronik*, 1485, plate 145, Municipal and University Library, Berne

So man zalt von gottes geburt 1400 plü Jare hat
der Iuner Graf von Safoi gros krieg mit etlichen
welschen herren ennert taurach an der seiterin
Vnd von jnen bitt wegen santen jn die Romn
Berin ein gros hilff mit einer paner Vnd
was venner Niklaus von dieszpach Also zugen
die von Berin zu Un wol viertzig mile Aber
bald darnach santen si jm hilff gen Sant Germau
wider djon hin jn damit hand dennocht die von
Berin einer herrschaft von Safoi vast gedienet Lu
welchs land vnd tarent das gen roam es Lnen vor
males ouch geholfen hat da si von aller menglichem
verlassen warent

28 Amongst beggars receiving alms there is a woman in the background.
Miniature from *Grandes Chroniques de France,* fifteenth century, Ms. fr. 2609, fol. 230 v. Bibliothèque Nationale, Paris

29 The illuminator uses the story of the Trojan Horse to illustrate the horrors of war in general, and in particular its dangers for women and children.
Book illustration in a version of Orosius, 'The Trojan Horse', ca. 1390/1410, Ms. fr. 301, fol. 147. Bibliothèque Nationale, Paris

30 Women entering Rostock through the Zingel gate; at the same time other women leave the town by coach.
Vicke-Schorler-Rolle, 1578/86, detail. Stadtarchiv Rostock

31 Depictions such as this give us an insight into the lives of women painters in the late Middle Ages. The daughter or wife of a painter was undoubtedly involved in helping to create a background or touch up a painting.
Miniature from Ms. fr. 12420, fol. 92 v., 1402. Bibliothèque Nationale, Paris

Cy apres lenfuit hystoire
de qireue femme de crai
na y val de rab riche

S lanoir mon
le yrene fut fe
me greque on
le par aage ve
qui longue
ment certam
nest pas toutevoies on croit
mienlx quelle fut creque et

tues comme bien parees homo
rees comme nobles comme pu
issantes et a plusieurs grans
dommages et plusieurs gns
prouffis de ceq si sont venus
et ensuis. ¶ Et pour certai
ne maudiroie lorgueil qui de
ce qi est ensin. se par les fem
mes ou leurs priers la fran
chise rommaine ne demou
rast. ¶ Mais la liberalite
du senat trop grande et trop
excessiue et la demeure par
rant de uecles moult donna
geuse ne pius loer. ¶ Car
contemptes de mendre dons
euscent este. ¶ Et bien po
uray sembloit tresgrant cho
se du temple fonde et en richy
a femmine fortune ¶ Mais
que pius ce estre le monde est
feminin et les hommes sont
femmins. ¶ Car pour cer
tain ce qui a este contraire
aux hommes et les choses mt
proffitables que le grant a
age si a destruittes na peu del
tiune ne a priuer le droit aux
femmes que garde ne la sent
tresfort et uertueusement.
¶ Les femmes adoncqs
a beturie rendirent loenges
et honnourerent son nom
et sa merite toutes les fois
que leurs cheueur quelles

ont moult chiers de pourpre et
dor sont atournez et que les
hommes quant elles passent
se lieuent contre elles et que
a elles opseules grans substa
ces seulent uenir de ceulx qui
meurent.

Cy deuise de thamar la
tresnoble paintre celle fil
le de mison. la lviij. rubriche.

hamar en so
temps et en so
aage fut tres
noble paintre
uelle et se il est
ainsi que le
grant temps nous ait oste
moult grandement de la sou
uenance de sa uertu et de son
bien. ¶ Toutuoies son
noble nom par la cause de so
artifice encore oster ne nous

32 Artist
painting a picture of
Mary. She also has
an assistant at her
disposal.
Miniature from Ms.
fr. 12420, fol. 86,
1402. Bibliothèque
Nationale, Paris

33 Woman paint-
ing a self-portrait.
Her simple working
clothes suggest she
is a professional
artist.
Miniature from
Ms. fr. 12420,
fol. 101 v., 1402.
Bibliothèque
Nationale, Paris

34 Women, bottom right of picture, in a chapel such as may have been found in a convent.
Illustration of Psalm 67, Ms. lat. 8846, fol. 114, thirteenth century.
Bibliothèque Nationale, Paris

ning of the following century, prosperous citizens founded a school fraternity here, in order to promote the further development of the town's school education. From 1518 onward women are listed among those members of the fraternity who made financial contributions. This, as well as the fact that the citizens of fifteenth-century Zwickau not only wrote letters and receipts but were also in a position to draft and even write out their own wills, leads us to the conclusion that women and girls were given a thorough grounding in the elementary subjects.

Apart from the elementary schooling provided by the church or the burghers, the daughters of less prosperous town inhabitants could choose another way to acquire the basic knowledge required for their professional life. In the fourteenth and fifteenth centuries, numerous so-called corner schools sprang up. Here women—commissioned only by the parents of the children—gave instruction in reading, writing, and arithmetic. Such small private schools existed, for example, in Strasbourg, Frankfurt on Main, Augsburg, Überlingen, Speyer, Stuttgart, Hamburg, Lübben, Breslau, Berne, Zurich, and Basle. A signboard by Hans Holbein the Younger advertising the services of a schoolmaster and schoolmistress in Basle who had opened such a private school has the following text: 'If there is anyone here, who would like to learn how to read and write in German in the shortest possible time, whereby anyone who previously did not know one letter of the alphabet can quickly master the basics, so that afterwards it will be possible to write and read whatever is due to him; and should anyone be too dull-witted to learn this, he will be taught for nothing and no recompense will be demanded, whether he be burgher or craft journeyman, woman or maiden. Whoever be in need of instruction should step inside and teaching will be given for a reasonable fee. The young boys and girls will, however, be admitted, as is customary after Ember days. 1516'.[25] Sometimes female shopkeepers, for example in Strasbourg, gave private lessons. Elderly women, for example in Hamburg, also took on some teaching of reading, writing, and arithmetic. There is evidence that the schoolmistresses could in some circumstances—presumably due to the fact that their teaching matter would be more related to practical life—represent competition to the male schoolteachers of the higher-level schools. This is seen in a contract drawn up between the schoolmaster of the Überlingen secondary school and the local female schoolteacher who gave private lessons. In order that the former did not suffer too much from the fact that some citizens wanted to send their children to Wantzenrutinin, the female schoolteacher had to undertake to pay him a certain amount for every boy pupil she took on per year.

The Brussels school decree of 1320 gives us some idea of the wages paid to the teaching staff in the town primary schools. According to the decree, male and female schoolteachers could both take 12 shillings' worth of coins for every pupil per year. About a third of this, however, had to be handed over to an official who acted as a type of headmaster.

If up till now we have only mentioned primary school education for girls, this is not because girls were generally excluded from higher-level education or from the Latin schools. In Brussels, according to the 1320 school decree, parents could send any number of their sons and daughters to the secondary school. It is doubtful whether girls could be prevented from overstepping the border to higher education in the course of time. It is, however, clear that in the Walloon town of Valenciennes, both girls and boys attended the Latin school. In Emmerich the 1445 contract obviously guaranteed girls access to the higher-level school. There is, however, little evidence of any practical effects. In all the European countries, even in Italy, the number of well-educated women outside of the religious orders who displayed a lively interest in science and politics remained extraordinarily low. On the rare occasions that we do come across such women—for example Heloise, the pupil, lover, and wife of Peter Abelard (1079–1142), the famous theologian and philosopher—we find that they were educated either by private tutors or by members of their own family.

The motivation behind campaigns to encourage female town inhabitants to learn how to read, write, and do simple arithmetic in the more important urban centres of the late Middle Ages—one is almost tempted to speak of a late Middle Ages literacy campaign—was primarily the requirements of town life, in particular the growing demands of trade and manufacturing, administration and public welfare.

Not only did the enlightened attitude toward primary education for girls lead women of the towns to become better equipped to participate in trade and craftwork at all levels; it also allowed them to take on more important duties in the service of the town community. Perhaps this was at the back of the mind of Sarah, a Jewish inhabitant of Görlitz, when in 1388 she donated a house that had been left by her to a fellow Jew, Isaac, to be used as a school for future generations of Jewish children.

* Since the qualifications required of teachers were comparable to those for German clerks, it should come as no surprise to find that women were also employed as clerks in the fifteenth century. One of the earliest records of women working as secular scribes comes from Basle, where, in 1297, a woman called Irwina was paid for making copies of documents. In the fourteenth and fifteenth centuries at least two more female clerks were employed in this town; others are known to have been employed in Cologne, Esslingen, Nuremberg, and Augsburg. A female clerk in Esslingen called Mechthild was married to a cloth shearer in the second half of the fourteenth century. It is known that Adelheid, another clerk from Esslingen, this time unmarried, not only had money and property but could employ a housekeeper and was thus in an ideal position to practise her profession. Another clerk, from Augsburg, Clara Hätzler, had her own studio from 1452 to 1476. In Nuremberg, the death registers of the St. Sebald parish for the years

1439–1517 provide evidence of specialisation within the profession. It records five female clerks, one female guilder scribe, three female clerks of court, three female tax clerks, and two female town council clerks. Probably all of them, with the exception of the guilder scribe, who seems to have been paid for each individual piece of work completed, were employed by the town council. (These five, like the male 'German clerks', probably also worked as teachers in the lower-level schools; there are fourteen female clerks recorded in the death register and only three female schoolteachers.)

Cologne had a particularly high number of women in the employment of the town council. Thus the High Court employed one female clerk (*Schryverse*) and a female assessor of pledges paid to the court. In Cologne it was very common for women to be sworn in at court in order to be employed as assessors. For the period around 1460 alone, eight are mentioned by name. It was the task of these so-called 'businesswomen' to assess assets and fines as well as to organise the sale of pledges in their stalls next to the mint and the delivery of the proceeds to the court. Female middlemen or brokers were also sworn in as town employees. They would store goods in order to sell them on behalf of others, usually foreign merchants. From the second half of the fourteenth century to the end of the following century, more than ten women were independently entrusted in Cologne with raising custom duty and road tolls. There are further records of women performing these tasks in the Saxon mining town of Freiberg in the fifteenth century, in Frankfurt on Main at the end of the fourteenth century, and in Augsburg and Innsbruck in the sixteenth century. Unlike Nuremberg, where the wife of the customs officer tended to be sworn in with her husband and was thus obviously only there to help see that things ran smoothly or to step in for her husband when necessary, the women mentioned previously were employed independently for these posts. A female farmer of customs could delegate her work to a son. It was also possible for a female farmer of customs to work for a male one. There are records of both such situations in Cologne.

The sources also mention cases, for example in Saxony and Cologne, of female customs officers or road toll collectors being robbed or assaulted. Yet a report dating from the mid-sixteenth century and written by a town council officer in Augsburg, which describes the work of a local female customs officer, presents quite a different picture. 'We have informed ourselves in the country and have found that the hunter's wife has a good reputation and has accomplished more [as a customs officer] with her good words than before, when there was much quarrelling and disagreement. She is also unbending in her attitude to the customs officer of the bishop, when he wants to introduce a new payment [for the benefit of his master] and does not want to permit this'.[26] Another service sometimes entrusted to women in the employment of the town community was that of the approved salt seller and measurer *(Salzmuter, Salzcherin)*. Thus the 1376 Pettau town law makes provision for twenty-four female salt traders. In Coblenz, too, the town salt trade was dominated by women. The same was true of the grain trade in Strasbourg, and we have already seen that married couples ran the grain trade in Marseilles. Women were found in other town offices—a female currency changer has already been mentioned. There are examples of females occupying the posts of tax collector, foundling-home officer, field guard, porter, tower guard, town keeper-of-the-keys, town musician, messenger of socage duties, and town shepherdess. Other posts were held jointly by married couples—bridge officer, and keeper or caretaker of the town measuring scales, the town hospital, the prison, the town general store, and the town house.

✳ There is evidence that women worked as illuminators in France, Germany, and the Netherlands. They embellished the individual letters and initials in the copies made of valuable books. This was certainly a continuation of an old convent tradition, but it became part of town artistic activity, because the master would, as a matter of course, fall back on the help of his wife and children. At the end of the thirteenth century a Paris book illustrator, Master Honoré, opened a school for book illustration in Paris with the help of his daughter and son-in-law. (The names of the daughter and son-in-law are not known.) In the fourteenth century the Parisian artist Jean le Noir introduced his daughter to the

Jugglers on the road.
Coloured woodcut by an anonymous artist, broadsheet, ca. 1450.
Herzog Anton Ulrich Museum, Brunswick

art of illumination. Another female book illustrator, Thomasse, worked in Paris around 1292, at the same time running an inn. High praise is given by writer Christine de Pisan to another illuminator working in Paris: 'I know a woman today, named Anastasia, who is so learned and skilled in painting manuscript borders and miniature backgrounds that one cannot find an artisan in all the city of Paris—where the best in the world are found—who can surpass her, nor who can paint flowers and details as delicately as she does, nor whose work is more highly esteemed, no matter how rich or precious the book is'.[27] In Cologne in the fourteenth century a married couple worked together as book illustrators, and in Lille there were female illustrators as well. One is recorded in Bologna as early as 1271. In Bruges, the secular miniature painter Grietkin Scheppers opened a workshop in a convent. In 1476 another woman from Bruges, Elisabeth Scepers, carried on the work of a workshop with the wife of her deceased teacher and in the same year was admitted to the artists' guild of the town.

Women in the west and southwest German towns were also employed in the handicrafts. They would paint playing cards and dolls, print letters, and do woodcarvings. In copies of antique works we often come across representations of female painters at their easels, a scene which is rooted in the environment of the late medieval town. This suggests that women also tried their hand at more elevated forms of art. On the whole, however, the female artist would be employed as auxiliary help in her father's or husband's workshop to do groundwork or to paint in areas that were already defined.

One area of female artistic activity not recognized by the town councils or the upper social strata of the towns was that of theatrical and musical performances. Only a very few female musicians and singers were given official approval. A singer and harp player was fetched by Wenceslas I, King of Bohemia, to play at his court, and a church singer was granted a daily wage by the Görlitz town council in the fifteenth century. Here and there one also finds mention of female town musicians. The majority of musically gifted women, whether they were dancers, acrobats, flute players, fiddlers, fife players, lute and cymbal players, carriers of Turkish jingles, or vielle players, had to make their living with the travelling performers, were ostracised from town society and liable to be persecuted as sorceresses or witches, and many of them lost their lives.

* And so we come to the darker side of women's employment outside the home, namely prostitution. Numerous women in the large and medium-sized trade and manufacturing towns made a living as prostitutes. Detailed studies of Florentine prostitution in the fifteenth century have shown that the brothels mainly recruited among foreign women or women from different towns. The sources give us no clue as to why these women chose this profession. Certainly the brothel owners and their agents would find it easier to tempt women in foreign countries with promises of an easy life, or to use deceit in order to entice them away from their homes. For many prostitutes, however, it was not always a matter of choice. Often relatives, foster parents, and sometimes their own parents would give the girls over to this profession when they were still children. The court records of big European trading towns such as Florence list cases in which women were accused of sending out their daughters to 'work'. In the medium-sized town of Mühlhausen (Thuringia) we find a court record of a female inhabitant being punished for sending her adolescent daughter to a brothel. The Mühlhausen town council rebukes one father for sending his under-age daughter to the 'marriage bed' with a stranger and records punishments meted out to the owners of brothels who had abducted children to work as prostitutes.

On the subject of prostitution, much has been written on the church's strikingly tolerant attitude toward it and the peculiar legal and social position of the prostitutes themselves. Reports exist of the high income of some of these 'beauties' who were clever enough to exploit meetings of the secular and church nobility, such as meetings of the German *Reichstag*, and church council meetings, as do reports of the brutal measures taken by such prostitutes to defend their privileges against unorganised competition. This approach has tended to trivialise the actual destitution of these women. Evidence of this is provided by the occasional mention given to brothel customers being punished for maltreatment of the women, as well as by the fact that the women would attend church services to try to escape their work, and would be accompanied by the brothel owner and his male servants on these occasions. In towns where prostitution was practised quite freely, guild statutes and town council regulations ensured that these women remained social outcasts. These included measures such as making them recognizable through their clothing, banning them from the drinking and social establishments of the town, and making them as invisible as possible by forcing them to live in housing on the outskirts of the town. On the whole, however, the attitude of the town councils toward prostitution was benevolent, and they tended to intervene only in cases of maltreatment of under-age girls (those under twelve years old). The councils encouraged the opening of brothels and most of the bigger towns had more than one. The councils also organised supervision of the brothels; in the Austrian towns this was one of the duties of the hangman. The reasons behind this attitude on the part of the councils are complex. The economic aspect was important. The income from these establishments represented a steady source of income for the town budget and found its way to the coffers of some burghers. They were therefore mainly concerned to suppress the underground, uncontrolled prostitution and the activities of pimps, unless this could be brought under council control. The income from brothels and the brothels themselves were sometimes donated to religious establishments and were even accepted by con-

A prostitute in Sicily, who has taken money from a young merchant, lends it back to him so that he can conduct his business. In: Albert Schramm, *Der Bilderschmuck der Frühdrucke.* Vol. IV. Leipzig, 1921, ill. 2908.

vents. This is true of a convent in Esslingen *(zum Kreuz Sirnau)*, which in 1433 charged two Stuttgart brothels an annual interest rate of one pound's worth of farthings, which, it must be said, was then passed on to others. Apart from their hopes of financial gain, the burghers and town councils were concerned to protect their own marriages and families from the nobility, celibate clergy, foreign merchants, and scholars. Such considerations lurk behind the generosity they showed toward prostitutes when the king and his entourage came on visits to the royal boroughs, and also explain the greater freedom prostitutes enjoyed in the towns that were either royal seats of residence or leading European trade centres. The town councils were moreover concerned to offer some sort of compensation for the marriage restrictions placed on journeymen and servants by the guilds and by individual masters. In the late Middle Ages married men were forbidden to set foot in brothels and the wealthier burghers would therefore exploit the dependent position of maids or, in the Mediterranean countries, of the slaves, to compensate for failed marriages or for their wives' repressed sexuality.

If we look back at the wide spectrum of female professional employment in the late Middle Ages and compare this to the position at the beginning of the commune movement, we find that in the four centuries from the second half of the eleventh century to the eve of the early bourgeois revolution, women's position as one of the family breadwinners was firmly established.

The demands of economic life in the late Middle Ages as trade was extended and intensified dictated that women participate at all levels in family trade. Sometimes this led to women taking over, should the family business be threatened due to the husband leaving his family, falling ill or dying, or should the husband prove to be unreliable or incompetent. A different development can be discerned in the crafts, which now had to meet the growing demand for export goods and for trade in mass consumption goods. As the division of labour between goods production and the sale of goods grew, the wives of masters and the maids became indispensable for the sales side of the business. The increasing social differentiation within and between the guilds, however, made it necessary for women from the crafts to look for a supplementary income or wage labour. Finally, women's economic independence led to at least a limited circle of the female town citizens' leaving the restricted world of their own homes to take part in the life of the town community. The entry of some women into town life was encouraged by the co-operative character of the trades and crafts guilds, which tended to incorporate the whole family.

We can find considerable confirmation for the above statements if we examine the role of women in town economic life from the point of view of the accumulation of wealth, or the proportion of women among the owners of mobile and immobile property and their ability to use this property gainfully in trading or craft activities. One decisive prerequisite for the many-sided involvement of numerous townswomen in the professional and economic life of the large and medium-sized towns was the considerable expansion of education facilities for women in the late Middle Ages. When girls began to be admitted to elementary schooling, the daughter of the average town burgher could more or less be guaranteed a minimum amount of education. Previously such burghers would not have been able to afford a private tutor or a convent school. This helped the daughters to develop skills and facilitated their entry to professional life.

Women's Position under Town Law and in Marriage and Family

For all women who were involved in some way or other in trade there were special legal arrangements made which covered an area from Italy via Switzerland, France, Germany, Flanders, and Denmark to England. It has already been mentioned that women operating independently could acquire citizens' rights in the late Middle Ages. This suggests a considerable divergence from the previous legal position of women as outlined in Chapter 1. Other changes, too, occurred in the legal status of women in towns from the end of the thirteenth century onward. How wide was the scope for a change in the legal position of women, once the medieval town was fully developed; and to what extent were the women's social status and their marital role affected?

✳ It is, of course, difficult enough to attain a consistent picture of the position of women in one town, let alone in a larger area, or indeed in all the leading states in medieval Europe. What follows are findings for the German-speaking parts of Europe, supplemented by examples from other European countries which are intended to point to parallel or specific developments.

Legal practice in European towns was based partly on prevailing legal theories as taught at universities and partly on records of regional juridical practice as contained in documents like the *Sachsenspiegel* and the *Schwabenspiegel* in Germany. In Italy and southern France, the shaping of law of the high Middle Ages was considerably influenced by Roman law, whereas in Germany this influence came from Frankish and Sax-

on law. Town law grew out of prevailing theory and records of legal cases, but also included elements of local common law. This was sometimes the case even when a fully developed legal system was handed down by one town to another—as often happened. Thus while there was a certain consistency of legal systems grouped around any town that had a significant legal tradition, there was still room for variation in the settling of basic questions. As there was no codified civil law in general, common law and law of contract—despite the increasing influence of Roman law—continued to play an important role.

Even when one has access to the information contained in municipal legal statutes and other records, one still does not necessarily have a reliable key to the actual juridical practice in the town concerned. Apart from the possibility of subjective interpretation of the laws, there is, especially where property matters are concerned, much scope for modification by means of individual contracts or wills—in particular the right of testament, which was enshrined in municipal legislation as an inalienable right of the individual.

✳ It is the legal position of married women that we will concentrate on, as one can assume that the majority of women in towns married, despite restrictions imposed by guilds and employers on journeymen, servants, and labourers, and despite the celibacy required of members of the clergy. In the towns there was a gradual change away from the early feudal system and toward the church system of both partners having the right to decide on marriage for themselves. This was expressed in the informal declaration of marriage by the priest, who symbolically brought together the hands of the bride and groom. This simple ceremony—which was only replaced by more elaborate forms in the sixteenth century—often took place in front of the doors of the church, making it a public declaration. This was necessary as a result of the spread of church marriage law, for once the principle of free marriage without the permission of parents, relatives, or guardians was announced, there was a spate of secret weddings. A relevant factor was the fact that, at least at the outset, parents and relatives were not prepared to refrain from viewing marriage as largely a matter of family interest.

The practice of secret marriages brought with it certain dangers for the principle of monogamy promulgated by the Catholic church, and meant an additional load for the church courts. Some figures will make this clear. Between November 1372 and May 1375 in Canterbury there were 78 cases to achieve recognition of marriages that had taken place in secret. Forty-one such cases were recorded in Paris between 1384 and 1387. One hundred of two hundred cases in Augsburg in 1350 were of this kind. About three-quarters of the plaintiffs were women, who usually were the ones who suffered most from such secret marriages, by defloration and pregnancy. In Regensburg in 1490 no fewer than 119 women brought cases for legalisation of such liaisons, damages, or alimony payments. In contrast to the Eng-

Marriage ceremony with priest, in the presence of witnesses. Woodcut, printed by Günther Zainer, Augsburg, 1477. In: Albert Schramm, *Der Bilderschmuck der Frühdrucke.* Vol. II. Leipzig, 1920, ill. 710.

Mutual consent to marriage in the presence of the king. The man and woman imitate the gestures of affirmation made by the king and in this manner declare themselves ready to submit to his judicial ruling.
Miniature from a French translation of the *Codex Justinianeus*, early fourteenth century, Ms. 392, fol. 66 v. Bibliothèque Municipale, Orléans

lish and French examples, judgements in favour of the plaintiff in Augsburg and Regensburg did not insist on the married couple sanctifying their marriage in church. It would appear that it was feared there would be resistance from the parents, relatives, masters, or employers. The town councillors almost always opposed marriages carried out without the agreement of the parents, relatives, and employers, and also marriages where the bride was abducted or eloped, which still occurred. Thus the town laws of Alès and Metz ordered that a woman could not take a husband without seeking the advice of her parents or guardian. In a number of towns, partners who decided upon marriage independently were punished when it came to inheritance: if they were not completely disinherited—as in Brünn and Leutkirchen—their in-

heritance might be withheld while the parents were still alive, or they might be banished for a year from the town and fined two marks, as in Mühlhausen (Thuringia). (In Brünn and Cracow it was only necessary for the daughter to receive permission to marry up to the age of 25. Thereafter she was free to act on her own will and was not fined for doing so.)

That there was a strong tradition of nonlegalised marriages can be seen from the statutes of Strasbourg in 1322. According to these, all those who lived 'openly in a state of marriage' within the city or the city precincts were exhorted to legalise their position. Those not prepared to do so, because one or the other had already married elsewhere, were to split up and divide their goods up between them according to the advice of the council. On separation, two-thirds of the children went to the man and one-third to the woman for further upbringing and education. Anyone who resisted this demand by the council had to reckon with sequestration of half his assets, 'in atonement for such a sin'.[28] At the same time the Strasbourg council was moved to take action against the worst form of bigamy, by threatening any man who took another woman into his house in addition to his wife with five years' banishment from the town. This also applied to the second woman. Men and women who kept their marriage secret and took another marriage partner were threatened with having their eyes put out. The fact that, despite such harsh penalties, illegal marriages continued, is proved by an agreement reached in Strasbourg in 1411 between master craftsmen and the town council which threatened all those who did not relinquish concubinage by the following Sunday with the sanctions contained in the town statutes. Cases where first marriages had been concealed or bigamy was openly committed were not rare; couples were continuing an unbroken tradition of the so-called *Friedelehe*. The additional statutes added to the Mühlhausen imperial law-book of 1351 to include contemporary legal practice explain how a woman can free herself of her partner simply by making a declaration to him before witnesses—which is precisely what was practised in a *Friedelehe*. In one case a New Year's gift is mentioned which only was to be given to maids and wives in a *Friedelehe*; otherwise the man was punished with an amount of one pound's worth of farthings or four weeks in prison. If we look at the laws on property and inheritance we see how secret marriage, which often was the only possibility which maids, journeymen, and servants had of living together, endangered not only the interests of families but also of women in the more wealthy classes.

✳ In the legislation covering the rights of property and inheritance within marriage the basic principle underlying feudal family law in central and western Europe was that of the man having sole powers of disposal. This principle spread, thanks to Italian legal scholars in the thirteenth century and, in the German-speaking world, contemporary writings, in particular the *Sachsenspiegel* and the *Schwabenspiegel*.

Both these books provided the basis for the legislation of many German towns. The *Sachsenspiegel* served as a model chiefly for towns that adopted Magdeburg laws, while the *Schwabenspiegel* was taken by towns in upper Germany. These books outline the husband's sole right to dispose of property and assets. Generally speaking, the man is confirmed as having the guardianship over the woman.[29] Above all this applies to assets: 'When a man takes a woman, he takes into his possession and acquires disposal rights over all her property.

Woman bathing in a tub and drinking from a goblet. A man is making music.
Woodcut, printed by Johann Blaubirer, Augsburg, 1481. In: Albert Schramm, *Der Bilderschmuck der Frühdrucke*. Vol. XXIII. Leipzig, 1943, ill. 727.

Priest and a woman in the stocks. The danger of adultery with a clergyman was particularly great, since he, as the person responsible for spiritual welfare, could exert influence over the psyche of the woman.

Marginal drawing from a copy of the *Smithfield Decretals*, early fourteenth century, Ms. Roy, 10 E IV, fol. 287 r. British Museum, London

For this reason no woman may make her husband a present of her property or moveable assets'.[30] This right of disposal even applies in the case of women marrying men of lower social status: 'Even if a man be not of the same birth as a woman, he nevertheless has rights over her and she is his equal and acquires his legal status if she enters his bed'.[31] If widowed, the woman returned to her old legal status. The man always had chief say in matters relating to goods and assets: 'A woman may also not give away any of her property without the permission of her husband, nor may she buy property nor dispose of *Leibgedinge* [personal assets made over to her for her lifetime] because he is also an owner of that property'.[32]

The law of inheritance according to the *Sachsenspiegel* gave the woman half the provisions, the dowry, and the *Morgengabe*—the gift she received from her husband after the wedding night. The latter could consist of animals or *Leibgedinge*. Possible elements in the dowry are named as being: 'all sheep and geese, boxes with curved lids, all yarn, beds, featherbeds, pillows, linen sheets, table-cloths, cloths, towels, bowls and candlesticks, linen and all female clothing, rings and bracelets, head-ornaments, psalters and all books used in church services, chairs and chests, carpets, curtains and tapestries and all ribbons. This is what belongs to the dowry. And various miscellaneous objects which', writes the author, 'I shall not enumerate, such as brushes and scissors and mirrors'.[33] The law as enshrined in the *Schwabenspiegel* gives the woman the right to inherit the *Morgengabe* and *Leibgedinge*, as well as the right to have the goods returned to her which she brought into the marriage.[34] Instead of the dowry, she has the right to inherit all moveable assets. Should there be any moveable assets the couple had acquired together the widow had a due claim to them. However, if her husband had left no other instructions in his will, these assets had to be shared with any children.[35] Thus in the *Schwabenspiegel*, guardianship over assets is already slightly modified, as the agreement of the wife had to be given to certain decisions of the husband.[36] According to widespread legal practice this applied to transfers of land.

If her husband was behaving irresponsibly with goods and property she had brought into the marriage, the woman could go to court with a representative of her own selection.[37]

Even some special cases were regulated in favour of the wife. Thus, for example, the *Sachsenspiegel* protected a widow who was pregnant in her full property rights until the child was born.[38] If a woman was legally separated she retained half the provisions, dowry, and *Leibgedinge*.[39] The latter also remained hers when her husband lost his assets because he committed a crime.[40] A woman who had been properly legally married had a certain security as regards property and inheritance, despite her husband's guardianship. In addition to this she was not, in the case of pregnancy, under the same additional moral pressure put on a woman living in secret marriage.

* As already mentioned, the town laws combined traditions handed down in the form of law-books with those of a more local nature. The Lübeck town laws of 1294 gave the woman the dowry that she brought into the marriage. In the case of childless couples the next heirs of the husband received half of what was left. According to Magdeburg law the widow was left her clothing and jewellery and the goods she had brought into the marriage. The husband's real estate and moveable assets went to the nearest relatives. The oldest law-book of the imperial city of Mühlhausen (1220) also gives the land property to the family of the deceased husband; but the wife could use the family property for her lifetime. These inheritance rights of the relatives were preserved through the fourteenth and fifteenth centuries in town laws such as those of Regensburg; here, after subtracting what the wife had brought into the marriage, the household goods and any jewellery, the church received a third of the residue and two-thirds went to the relatives. In Constance, from 1472 onward, relatives of the deceased received one-third of the assets of the couple. Strasbourg law gave the relatives half the inheritance.

On the other hand, in Ulm and Göttingen, control of the entire inheritance went to the wife in the case of childless couples.

In the case of couples with children, the principle applied to both men and women that the survivor took personal property from the estate—the woman, her clothing and jewellery; the man, the *Hergewäte*, his personal clothes and breastplate, all his weapons and armour. There was variation from town to town in what the women could retain. All the rest passed in equal amounts to the surviving partner and relatives of the deceased. Usually no differentiation was made between children of a first marriage and those of a second. Distribution of the inheritance occurred when the children came of age (boys usually between 12 and 14, girls between 11 and 12), or married, or when they left the parental home—sometimes years after they had married. But town laws sometimes also specifically laid down that distribution among the children had to take place before the surviving partner remarried, or later changes could only occur with agreement of the children or their guardians.

The marital and property rights of men were largely retained in town laws. Thus, for example, the Mühlhausen imperial law-book *(Reichsrechtsbuch)* gives a narrow interpretation of the rights of the man and his nearest relatives, inasmuch as the son of the deceased, whether he be from that marriage or from another, had the right of guardianship over the widow. The husband's guardianship over the person and the property of his wife was also retained in Magdeburg and Lübeck. This had far-reaching consequences, as these towns influenced the law in regions beyond the borders of the medieval German state. But for some towns, such as Schlettstadt, Göttingen, Munich, Esslingen, Brakkenheim, Nuremberg, Constance, and Hamburg, the rights of the husband only covered assets. A regulation passed by the imperial city of Esslingen for Brakkenheim, in Württemberg in 1280, gives a short and to-the-point summary of the situation: 'The man could give all that he and his wife had . . . [whether they had children or not] personal goods, a fief or moveable assets to whomsoever he wished. Neither the wife nor the child nor the heirs had any right of appeal'.[41]

The number of towns whose laws deviated from these basic principles seems to have been very limited. Only Cologne, Regensburg, and Munich, among the larger German cities, did not spell out the husband's guardianship rights, while the position in Ulm, Göttingen, and Constance was not entirely clear. Very little information is found in the town laws about divorces. These were largely a matter for the churches, and were only occasionally dealt with among inheritance matters by the town councils of Göttingen, Zwickau, and Erfurt in the fifteenth century.

It should be noted that the majority of town laws, at the latest by the fourteenth and fifteenth centuries, guaranteed widows a significant portion of the inheritance (a third, a half or two-thirds of the total). In marriages with children, the mother, if she did not remarry, was allowed to use the children's portion of the inheritance, at least until they came of age. This was undoubtedly to the woman's advantage, for she thus enjoyed the fruits of what had been earned or acquired during the marriage. Widows from well-off families were thus guaranteed an adequate standard of living if their husband died early, and this was supplemented in many cases by the acquisition of life annuities. A fatherless family had sufficient funds to pay for schooling or an apprenticeship for the children, mainly the sons, and the woman could perhaps take up work of her own. On the other hand, town laws, with few exceptions, maintained the husband's right of guardianship over his wife during the marriage, at least in matters of inheritance—which surely led to difficulties: How could the wife of a merchant take on legal responsibilities for her husband during his frequent absences? How could the wife of a craftsman look after local sales if she was not able to collect debts herself and, if necessary, sue for payment? How could a linen weaver supply herself with thread if she was not allowed to apply for credit without a guardian? How could the wife of any burgher invest money on behalf of her family at good and safe interest rates without rights to dispose of assets? And, finally, how could an innkeeper store her customers' wares, carry out business, or lend money against security?

Again, solutions to such problems varied from town to town. In Basle in the second half of the thirteenth century the woman gained full rights over real estate from the *Morgengabe*. Yet the fact that common rights over assets of the married couple were recognized did not lead to the woman having equal inheritance rights. The husband retained chief rights, despite the fact that the wife increasingly shared responsibility for legal transactions. Basle town law provided for the husband to inherit two-thirds, the wife one-third of the total inheritance. This covered what had been acquired during the marriage. According to Viennese law the woman had a right to half the inheritance. But neither in Vienna nor in Basle, neither in north German Hanseatic towns nor in central German towns was this consistent practice.

In the late Middle Ages marriage contracts (agreements), property or annuities transfers, and special provisions in the wills of the husband or the woman's blood relatives provided important ways and means of women building up assets over which they had more or less complete control. Marriage contracts had, for families with considerable wealth or social prestige, special significance. Often the future husband was a member of a high social stratum within the urban bourgeoisie—for example, burghers with feudal fiefs, families from whose ranks the town councillors were chosen, or families with mining businesses—and by marrying their son to a rich heiress from the burghers the family hoped to improve their financial position or solve a passing financial crisis. In such a social constellation the parents of the bride will have put emphasis on securing their daughter's situation.

Light is thrown on such considerations by a retrospective cross-examination of a witness by the town judges of Zwickau. In the marriage arranged between Frau Anna and Jorg Montzer, the latter's brother, Hanss Montzer, had made the following commitment to his future sister-in-law: If her husband did not provide for her he would give her 200 Rhenish guilders out of his own pocket, so that her future was assured. The members of the council and burghers who were questioned confirmed under oath in 1487 that this was the arrangement which had been made.

Marriage contracts, when signed by two people of equal social standing, secured a certain independence for each partner in property matters. This comes out in the contract signed in 1483 for Elspeth Rauhenperger of Salzburg and the Viennese burgher Blasius Ennglhartsteter. It laid down the dowry and *Morgengabe*, which, according to Viennese law, usually amounted to 300 pounds and 250 pounds of the best currency, respectively. All goods other than the dowry which the woman brought into the marriage the husband was to have, use, and enjoy. But the highly significant innovation was the following restriction: the husband had to guarantee that his wife could dispose of her assets as she wished, by selling, transferring, or donating them, or by giving them away 'without the intervention or interference of Ennglhartsteter's, her husband, or his heirs or any other person'. The same rights are given to the husband. Other contracts, wills, and transfers of assets—above all an enormous number of life annuity agreements made for both partners or for the wife alone—guaranteed for the wife assets over and above the usual one-third inheritance. In addition to the aforementioned annuities these could take the form of additional real estate, a single cash payment, jewellery, artefacts made of precious metals, or other objects. In some wills the wife even is given a half, rather than a third share of the inheritance, lifetime guarantees against claims by her children, or claims by her husband's relatives if she should receive the entire inheritance. Total mutual inheritance seems to have occurred mainly among craftwork couples where the partners worked independently

or where there was a division of labour between manufacture and selling—a relative rarity in centres of long-distance trade such as Lübeck, Bremen, and Stralsund, where the relatives' inheritance rights were important. Among traders the extended family needed to remain close-knit even beyond the confines of one town or region in a way that was not so necessary for those involved in craftwork, among whom, it develops, family businesses were relatively short-lived, which was even further aggravated by the travelling of the journeymen in the late Middle Ages.

Many late-medieval towns offer examples of wives who had partial control over the family's assets: Erfurt, Halle, Magdeburg, Halberstadt, Eger, Bamberg, Görlitz, Vienna, Sterzing, Basle, Genoa, Venice, Nuremberg, Regensburg, Cologne, Lübeck, Bremen, Ghent, and many others. These examples cover more than just those women who ran independent businesses or practised a craft. Even in England, where, as we have already seen, women could work independently only when they were regarded for legal purposes as unmarried, the husband could give his wife verbal authority to carry out certain matters relating to property. In Italy, where the tradition of Roman law gave particular emphasis to the position of the husband as head of the family, partial rights for the woman over the family assets were guaranteed by special laws covering assets—that is, parts of the dowry or inheritances of various kinds. As wives gained greater control over family assets, they were able to take part in transactions on the town securities market, play a role in business, and even operate independently in the trading sector.

* According to town laws unmarried women and widows usually had full rights over assets and the freedom to carry out legal transactions independently. Exceptions to this occurred only when the town council feared the possibility of assets getting into the hands of the church or the hands of outsiders who did not have citizens' rights. The council of Dortmund decreed that

Elisabeth Honiss, burgher and merchant, has her will drawn up legally in 1470 by the public notary. At bottom left, the mark of the notary's office. Extract from document no. 1122. Stadt- und Kreisarchiv Mühlhausen/Thuringia

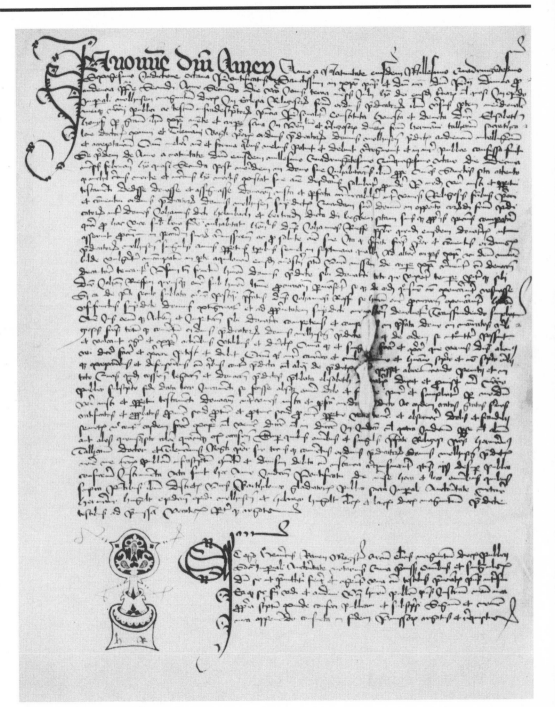

In a will drawn up in 1438, Elisabeth Grossen, a burgher of Mühlhausen, bequeaths a house behind the All Saints' Church to the mendicant friars of the Dominican Order. Extract from document no. 849. Stadt- und Kreisarchiv Mühlhausen/ Thuringia widows and parentless spinsters receive a guardian only when the council or the relatives deemed it necessary to preserve the assets and for the good of the heirs. In Strasbourg, in 1322, unmarried women and widows who possessed land were given men of good reputation from among their relatives as stewards. Relatives with rights of inheritance were excluded. If no suitable person could be found among the blood relatives, it was further stated, the council would appoint a steward. These stewards, quasi-guardians, had the task of ensuring that no annuities or possessions be removed and put to ordinary use. The women concerned should only receive the interest accruing from their assets. In cases of particular hardship the spinster or widow had the right to appeal to the council.

On the whole, however, without the need for a guardian, or with a legal representative whom they had themselves chosen (a development from the steward during the fourteenth century), women were able to sign contracts and acquire or pass on property and land. This covered, among other things, mills, shares of mills, brickworks, and market stalls. Women also received user's rights of various kinds either as women's fees for their lifetime or as men's fee that was inheritable. This included annuities from town offices, income from customs and the courts, shares in the town mint, in mines, salt springs, grazing and arable land, and fruit gardens. Various wills give an impressive picture of the assets that female heirs possessed. An outstanding example, inasmuch as it was drawn up and written entirely by herself—which illustrates the level of education achieved by an inhabitant of what was a highly successful mining and cloth trade town—is the 1469 will of Anna Truhenschmidt, a citizen of Zwickau. The document confirms indirectly the existence in Zwickau of the principle of the one-third inheritance: the widow makes frequent reference to the third she received from her husband. In addition to paying the family of her dead son Paul a certain share of the inheritance in advance, she mentions a daughter, Maidalen, a widow with three

daughters and three sons. This daughter, who, with the guardianship of two burghers, has the task of acting as executor of the will, receives an annuity of 20 guilders per year, which Anna acquired by paying 1,200 guilders to the Nuremberg council. If this daughter remarries, the son-in-law is excluded from benefitting from the annuity. Maidalen, who as executor is required to meet any outstanding debts, also receives the remaining assets. Another daughter, Martha, is already dead. She received 500 gold guilders for the purchase of an annuity of 25 guilders a year from the Nuremberg council. Her five children receive a further 300 guilders under Anna's will, which are also to be invested for annuities. The writer of the will assumes that the Nuremberg son-in-law will deny the inheritance. Her poor opinion of him can also be seen from her statement that the bed-linen which went with the daughter is requested to be returned and will become part of the final assets disposed of after the death of the writer.

Not having a large fortune at her disposal, Anna makes modest donations—between 2 and 30 guilders—to the fraternity of cloth makers, shopkeepers, the religious fraternities of the *Heilige Leichnam* and *Kaland* in Zwickau, and the Franciscans of Nuremberg. Just as the family of this citizen of Zwickau acquires annuities in Nuremberg, so many other female burghers from other towns invested sums in the town of Zwickau. Receipts in the Zwickau archives identify them as coming from Nuremberg, Eger, Freiberg, Oschatz, Eisleben, Rochlitz, Leipzig, Halle, and, of course, Zwickau itself.

The regulations in many towns for widows and widowers who wished to remarry proved to be a major factor preventing families of town citizens from accumulating large sums. Inheritance allowances were usually lost if the widow 'put away her widow's chair', as remarrying was described in wills. Sometimes the family house had to be vacated for the children, who would be represented by one or more guardians. As often as not, though, the widow's share of the inheritance was reduced to the same as the children's. In many towns, all matters of children's inheritance had to be settled before the surviving partner remarried and he/she was reduced to the same share as the children. This was bound to have an effect on people's marriage plans; the chronicle of Tilesio of Mühlhausen (late sixteenth century) states: 'In the year 1336 here in Mühlhausen the arbitrary and onerous statute was applied whereby fathers or mothers were not allowed to take more of their goods than the children's share of the inheritance. This reduced many a man to poverty. Many were also thereby discouraged from remarrying'.[42]

These practices may well have been one reason for the attitude, particularly in wealthy families, held toward newborns, which can only be described as careless. A baby was often entrusted to nurses who by no means guaranteed proper care for the infant. The regulations on children's inheritance rights before remarriage were not designed to increase a family's interest in having a large number of children. In craftsmen's families, as, for example in the Saxon textile centre of Chemnitz, the stepfather or stepmother often used the money the children had inherited for the necessary day-to-day expenses of the business. The children were given a piece of arable land or a house as security and to satisfy the laws of the town.

* The majority of unmarried or widowed women—who constituted between 8 and 38 percent of the town's taxpayers—were of interest to the town councillors mainly in terms of how their assets could be used for the town budget.

These women, as members of local families, shared indirectly the citizens' rights of their fathers or husbands. A widespread common law stated that the rights of the deceased husband passed to the widow—even in England, where women were allowed to join guilds but were categorically denied the right to acquire citizens' rights. In a few rare cases the councillors demanded that the widow and those of her children who were of age take the oath. In Schlettstadt the law demanded that the

widow of a citizen who had lived outside the town walls take over her husband's rights within a month of his death; otherwise she could only receive such rights 'as though she had never been a citizen'—in other words, she would get no special treatment. Strasbourg town law of 1322 appears to have been directed more at young people. Men and women aged 20 are called upon to be sworn in as citizens if their main domicile and their most valuable property are in town, whether or not they live with the father, mother, or relatives. Clearly this statute takes into account the fact that young married people often lived for years under the same roof as the parents and single women often lived with relatives. But it did not cover the considerable number of unmarried or widowed women and those fleeing from unfortunate marriages who were moving in increasing numbers to town. These were not just relatively poor women, such as maids, nurses, and wayfaring people, but often those who had sufficient wealth to earn their own living from trade or craftwork. These women, according to the laws of medium- and large-sized towns in the German-speaking countries, were obliged to take up independent citizens' rights. The Zwickau statutes of the fourteenth century make this very clear.

According to Zwickau law, a wealthy woman who moves to town without intending to marry must apply for citizenship. If the move occurs because of a marriage she receives the husband's rights 'if she enters his bed'. The Mühlhausen (Thuringia) law-book states much the same thing. The Schlettstadt laws of the end of the fourteenth century, mentioned elsewhere in this book, demand of all who move to the town to live and settle there that they become within a month of their arrival either a *Bürger* (citizen) or a *Seldener* (citizen with reduced rights) in order to serve the town and to remain obedient. Everyone—man or woman—is expected to enter a guild and serve it. The notion of 'service' would appear to apply to the town watch service and the defence of the town, which were organised by the guilds. All those who fail to meet this requirement receive no help and enjoy none of the rights and freedoms of the town of Schlettstadt. The town of Miltenberg required of men and women who acquired citizens' rights 3 guilders or a crossbow of the same value; however, it encouraged a rapid growth of its citizenry by waiving this payment for all outsiders who married into town families. An agreement between Lindau and Isny reveals that both towns accepted female citizens of the other town as their own citizens, thus following the principle 'town air makes one free'. If the woman moving into one town intended to marry, she had to have had citizens' rights in the other town for six weeks and two days. The same in reverse, incidentally, held for the husband.

Acquisition of citizens' rights involved the payment of a fee and the taking of a vow. For women, too, the duty of paying taxes and serving the watch and defence of the town were involved. The latter duties could be carried out by proxy or replaced by a special payment. Such an arrangement for female citizens can be seen, for example, in Erfurt, where in 1357 the council recorded that Gysela von Mittelhusen and Ermengard von Ilmene were, for the duration of their life and residence in Erfurt, 'released from all payments and watch duties on the walls and all other services which citizens have to provide, because they have given the town 19 pounds and 6 shillings' annual duty'.

Citizens books, which contain the names of all new people acquiring rights—those from Soest, Lübeck, Cologne, Frankfurt on Main, Freiberg (Saxony), Berlin, Stralsund, Dortmund, Strasbourg, Nuremberg, Dresden, Görlitz, Memmingen, Northeim, Emmerich, Fulda, and Reval are extant—show that cases of women acquiring citizens' rights were by no means isolated. The list for Soest between 1302 and 1449 contains the

Citizens' registers from the town of Stralsund record the names of women who were granted citizens' rights—Tilse Calen, Wobbeke Langhe, Katherina de Lobeze, etc.
Extract from the second oldest citizens' register of the Hanseatic town of Stralsund, 1349–1571, fol. 33b (1385). Stadtarchiv Stralsund

names of 5,623 citizens, of which 345 (that is, over 6 percent) are women. In Stralsund the figures for 1370 to 1373 reveal a proportion of over 5 percent. In Cologne between 1356 and 1399 only 3 percent of the new citizens were women; in the fifteenth century there were even fewer. Strasbourg took on 8 percent in 1452, and then, in 1459, 9 women out of 79 applicants. On the other hand, there were years when the proportion of women was under 1 percent or when none at all were taken on.

The women who had acquired citizens' rights had special privileges over those 'ordinary' inhabitants who had no such rights, although they were still excluded from council elections. A Görlitz Jewess, Adasse, mentioned in 1348 as the possessor of a promissory note for 71 marks, was one of the main town creditors. In Graz some Jewish widows were members of a financial syndicate, and in Vienna two Jewish women ran a public laundry with female paid workers. In Mühlhausen another Jewish businesswoman negotiated a settlement for herself, her husband, and her heirs concerning some goods that had been taken from them. Women could carry out legal business, complete contracts, act as guarantors, witnesses, executors, and sometimes as guardians for children or grandchildren. They could go to court to secure their property and could pursue debts in courts in other towns, without a guardian but with the support of their town council. This support from the council also was forthcoming for day-to-day legal affairs, to protect female citizens from prosecution in ecclesiastical courts, in cases where the husband had been deceitful in matters of property, or where marriage contracts and vows were concerned. Property contracts were completed by female citizens in Mühlhausen (Thuringia), Zwickau, Görlitz, and Stralsund. In the latter town women are mentioned eleven times between 1370 and 1382 as guarantors in affairs concerning citizens' rights.

In Nuremberg, on the other hand, this only occurred ten times between 1302 and 1448. In Zwickau, Mühl-hausen, and Stralsund women were cross-examined as witnesses in inheritance and property matters. In the previous chapter we have already mentioned the role of women as court witnesses in matters concerning securities. Women executors are mentioned in the Zwickau, Regensburg, Wiener Neustadt, Cologne, and London records. Mothers or grandmothers acted as guardians for children or grandchildren in Freiberg, Chemnitz, Zwickau, Halle, Görlitz, Nuremberg, and the French town of Périgueux.

The sometimes considerable wealth of female citizens brought tax advantages, for if the women made substantial private loans to the council or passed on coveted fiefs they could be granted exemption from paying taxes for several years. Such an arrangement was made by the widow of Herman von Levede, of Goslar, who for four years beginning in 1373 formally gave up interest payments due to her from the steward's office in return for tax exemption during the same period. She had only to remain living in Goslar; in addition to this she was to receive each week a shilling in Goslar pfennigs. Similar examples can be found in Görlitz and Lübeck.

Records show that in times of economic prosperity and labour shortages for certain urban professions, citizens' rights were used as a demographic device and bestowed even upon less wealthy arrivals, including women.

And there is evidence that councils filled the town coffers by raising money from maids who moved to the towns. Generally speaking, however, the same applied to citizens' rights as applied to property rights: they gave many women the necessary encouragement and support to enter town life more fully, whether the rights were acquired through the husband or, in the case of unmarried women, independently. On the whole, only women from the upper strata of society or from the wealthy middle classes could meet the requirements laid down by the councils for the acquisition of the full citizens' rights—by paying taxes punctually or purchasing proxies for watch and defence services.

✳ In his *Wanderbüchlein* Johannes Butzbach gives a description of an incident that occurred between his usually very cooperative stepfather and his mother. The cause of the incident was Johannes' decision to return to his studies. 'My father', he writes, 'was not a little pleased at this decision and immediately put the money for the journey at my disposal. He gave me five guilders. He also knew that my mother had a good guilder from her dowry which was called her own; with it he had become engaged to her. With all forcefulness he demanded that she give it to me. But my mother did not wish to hand it over. Instead she had given me another guilder behind my father's back. The matter soon became the cause of a lively argument between the two which ended in his beating my mother and pulling her hair. When I observed this I threw down my pack and the money

An adulteress is punished privately. She is tied to a pillar and forced to spend a sleepless night, while her husband sleeps soundly.
Woodcut, printed by Hans Hauser, Ulm, 1483. In: Albert Schramm, *Der Bilderschmuck der Frühdrucke.* Vol. VII. Leipzig, 1923. ill. 55.

and, together with my brother and sister, hurried to her aid. I managed to drag her away from him. . . . My father calmed himself. When he had come to his senses he started to be racked by his conscience. He hastened through the town in search of me. When he had found me he begged me from the bottom of his heart not to give up my resolve. He also entreated me to forgive the sin he had committed out of his desire to be good to me. So saying he handed me the guilder which he had forced into his possession by his violence. For the sake of peace I accepted it, but later returned it secretly to my mother, who had accompanied me to the ship'.[43]

Such a scene, occurring as it did in a family of by no means badly-off craftsmen, was no isolated case. Court reports from late-medieval towns contain countless judgements in cases where wives had been mistreated by their husbands, blood relatives, or even strangers. Wives' or their relatives' complaints ranged from her being threatened with a knife, beaten, turned out of the house to rough treatment by the husband's relatives and strangers invading the family home. There are cases of both women and men murdering their spouse. This sort of situation has to be seen as proof of the discrepancy that existed between the increased importance of female town dwellers in economic life and the continued survival of patriarchal attitudes toward the role of women within the marriage, the origins of which can be found in legal tradition and, as we will see, in religious ways of thinking.

Those town laws that for a long time preserved the husband's predominance over the woman in the form of guardianship also gave him the right to beat her—sometimes merely forbidding an excess of blows. The husband could pay off debts by selling his wife's belongings—coat, veil, pillows, jewellery. A case was recorded in Mühlhausen of a woman's only coat being pawned. If the wife was caught *in flagranti* breaking her marriage vows the law sanctioned brutal measures, right down to murder. In Dortmund a man who had murdered his wife and fled from the town afterward was allowed to retain not only his inheritance but that of his dead wife.

Cases of rape brought before the law were dealt with in a manner that almost always operated in the man's favour. The following statute was found in the Mühlhausen imperial law-book: 'If a man lie with a woman against her will and without her agreement, and she be thereby importuned, she should defend herself by crying out and should immediately report the matter with torn clothing, with wringing of hands and with weeping and with dishevelled hair'. If this occurs all persons should follow her to the judge, 'wherever he be found'.[44] Only seldom were the two witnesses required forthcoming. A respected citizen could easily, with the help of the council, silence any accusations against him, while the woman—who usually was from humbler social circumstances—found it much more difficult to defend her reputation.

As far as actual jurisdiction was concerned it is important to differentiate between the treatment meted out to female citizens and that given to members of the lower strata, noncitizens, and others. Criminal cases were treated in a manner very much against the interests of the accused if the latter was a rather poor inhabitant of the town without citizens' rights, and of course most punishments, with the exception of the death penalty, could be deflected by financial means. Town courts displayed particular cruelty (not just toward women; it was a general feature of medieval justice) in cases of theft, often irrespective of the value of the goods stolen. In Nuremberg and Augsburg during the years 1461, 1500, and 1503, three women found guilty of theft were buried alive. The Stralsund legal records register similar punishments for 1507 and 1513. Some women were drowned. In Görlitz, Freiberg, and Zwickau punishment could consist merely of banishment from the town for life. Judges showed particular harshness in their treatment of women in cases with political significance or those in which an example was to be made for others. In 1378, Agnes von Virbeke of Dortmund was burned as a sympathiser of the aristocracy, which was hostile to the town.

In marriage courts, which some councils set up in competition with the ecclesiastical courts, it appears that judgements had to take into account the rapid spread among all strata of unregulated sexual relations. Court records from Görlitz during the years 1370 and 1447 (*Liber proscriptionum* II) are very explicit on this: 'There are in the whole of Görlitz but few married people, fewer than twelve, who are not guilty of adultery; if one were to pillory all adulterers here in Görlitz then the new market place would be far too small to accommodate them all'.[45] Such a situation probably is the explanation for the ruling on illegitimate children made by the councils of Constance and Regensburg. In Constance a woman who had a child by an unmarried man could put the child in his care, but the child would not have inheritance rights. In Regensburg the mother always had the right to give the father an illegitimate child to care for a year after its birth. Clearly the council, by this ruling, was attempting to do something about the large number of foundlings who, in the end, were a strain on the town budget. A mother who killed her child was dealt with without mercy and without any thought to her partner—she was drowned or burned. Similarly, a woman who was proved to have killed her husband was punished by death.

✳ Does this gloomy picture of the relationship between the sexes inside and outside marriage, gleaned largely from law-books, court judgements, and general historical records, give an accurate reflection of everyday life in the late Middle Ages? To answer this question it is necessary to look at other sources of information—literary, autobiographical, and pictorial accounts. And in fact, we find that the negative examples portrayed above are balanced by many cases of close and harmonious relations within marriages and families. Certain women from the patriciate—like the wife, mother, and sister of the Munich chronicler Jörg Kazmair, who came into conflict with the council in 1398—went to extremes to preserve the wealth and reputation of their family.

They tackled the council themselves and risked being transported out of the town with a stone round their necks—a punishment reserved for rebellious and slanderous women. Their arguments used before the council reveal that they were not acting under Jörg Kazmair's guardianship but were themselves clearly knowledgeable in legal matters.

Many solemn oaths and attestations (*Verschwörbriefe* and *Urfehdebriefe* in German) from citizens arrested and condemned by councils and forbidden to enter the town and do any ill to its citizens were specifically required to be signed by the wife. In some cases such documents reveal that the wife was involved in activities directed against the council and therefore had to share the imprisonment. In the internal feuding that beset Halle between 1478 and 1479 women from the ranks of the wealthy salt panners were put under house arrest because they had joined their husbands in revolting against the council.

What can be said about the women from the upper strata goes for the wives of the guild craftsmen and merchants. Here, too, many wives gave loyal and steadfast support to their husbands when they were involved in municipal or commercial affairs. The wife of Johannes Mauersperling of Halberstadt, when her husband was unsuccessful in a lawsuit against the St. Paul's seminary, herself pursued the matter through the town courts. The subject of the dispute was her property rights over a stand near the graveyard of St. Martin's church. Because her husband did not accept the judgement he was excommunicated, and for her pains the Halberstadt ecclesiastical authorities threatened her with a similar punishment.

On a number of occasions women in the Saxon mining town of Freiberg joined their husband, son, or daughter in protesting against guilds and council. An interesting example is that of the Deynhard family. It was said of the wife of Deynhard, the Deynhardinne, that she had said 'unseemly words' to citizens in the council chamber and had refused to return one of their weapons.

Reinfried and another member of the family were also punished for disobedience and unseemly words toward the council. The same happened to the stepson of Reinfried Deynhard in 1427.[46]

In Brunswick the role played by wife and family emerges in the revolt of Ludeke Hollant against the council between 1487 and 1499. After the execution of a conspirator, the shopkeeper Wolter Holthusen, his betrayer felt so threatened by the wives of some of the rebels that he managed to have them banned from the town. Some of those banned were 'Wolter Holthusen's wife, Ludeke Ereke's wife with her daughter, and Jasper Bossen's wife and Kersten Flugge's wife and various other women'. The wife of Holthusen (who had been gruesomely executed) did not let the matter rest there. She lodged a claim of unlawful killing and dispossession of her house and property with the curia in Rome and thus managed to have the council called to Rome to account for itself.

Women played a prominent part above all when there was an external threat to the town. This can be seen from Adolphus of Nassau's report of the taking of Mainz, from which the burghers' wives were banished with only the clothes they wore, because they had thrown stones at the enemy and poured hot water over them from their houses.

According to one report by Cafarus, the men and women of Genoa worked day and night to build up the defence structures of their town when, after the Imperial Diet of Roncaglia in 1158, an attack by the Emperor Frederick I seemed imminent. No less significant is female involvement in times of emergency, as recorded in the diary of an anonymous citizen of Paris dating from the first half of the fifteenth century. According to this diary the wives and daughters of Paris citizens went to the wife of the regent, the duchess of Burgundy, and asked her to help restore peace. She apparently replied that this was also her greatest desire, and assured them that the duke was determined to do his utmost to achieve peace, suggesting that the Paris women presented their case well. The peace treaty of Arras signed in the same year by the duke of Burgundy and King Charles VII allowed joint action to be taken against the English occupying forces and represented a turning point in the Hundred Years' War (1337–1453) between England and France.

There are examples of men standing up for wives who have come into conflict with the law or broken with societal norms. Thus we find that Merten Helbig, a Görlitz master clothmaker, followed his wife, who was banished from the town as a punishment for a theft she had committed two years previously. A Görlitz tailor, Frantz Hiller, whose wife had left with a journeyman because she had been mistreated, took her in again, even though this brought him into conflict with the guild, which excluded him from their ranks for his action. The chancellor of the king of Bohemia pleaded with the council that the pair should be allowed to remain in Görlitz, but the guild was unmoved. Hiller protested against the mayor of the town, was arrested, and had, with his wife, to swear an oath never to return and finally leave town. In Mühlhausen (Thuringia) in the early fifteenth century five citizens swore an oath in support of Tile Vorsprache, who had been called before the council on account of a statement he was alleged to have made to the effect that he would avenge his wife if harm befell her in the town prison.

Such examples show that in a situation where men and women were functioning both economically and socially as partners, it was possible for deep human relationships to develop. These first beginnings of a new concept of love and marriage are well expressed in the first words in Geoffrey Chaucer's *Franklin's Tale* of his *Canterbury Tales*:

35 First page of the third municipal record of Stralsund, in which transfers of property to, or by women are recorded.
Liber de hereditatum venditione et resignatione, 1385–1418, fol. 1.
Stadtarchiv Stralsund

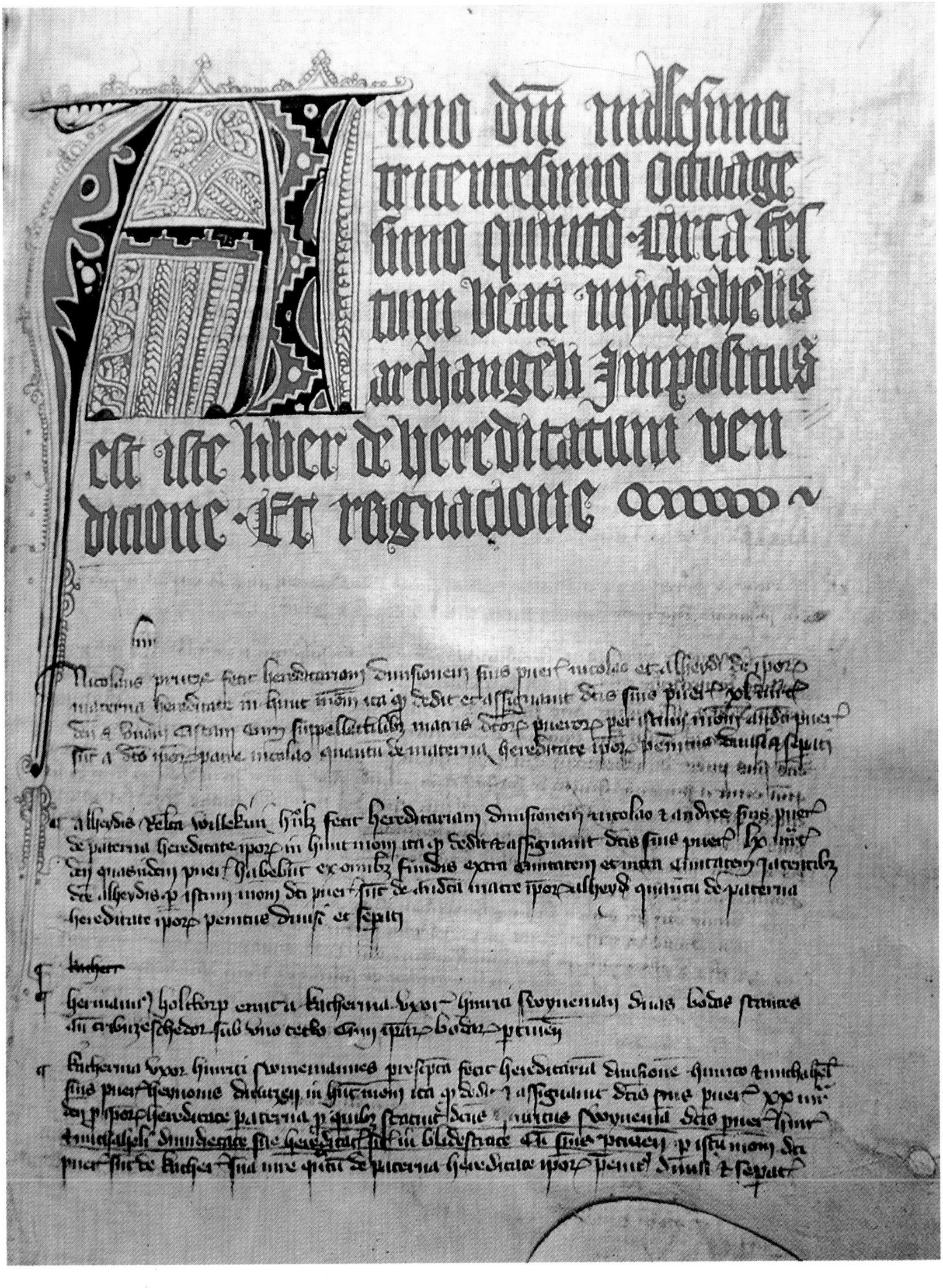

Anno dñi millesimo
triceñtesimo octuage=
simo quinto · circa fes=
tum beati mychabelis
archangeli Impositus
est iste liber de hereditatuni ven
diaõne · Et ragnaõone ◊◊◊◊◊◊ ~

Nicolaus pruce fecit hereditariam diuisionem suis pueris Nicolao et Alheydi de pos...
...materna hereditate in hunc modum ita q̃ dedit et assignauit suis pueris pre...
...et Buden castrum cum suppellectilibus mauis deorp pueros per istum modum...
...suis de suo ipsorum parte mealo quanto de materia hereditate ipsorum penitus diuisa ...

...Alheydis relca wilkelm hinz fecit hereditariam diuisionem nicolao z andres suis pueris
de paterna hereditate ipsorum in hunc modum ita q̃ dedit z assignauit suis pueris...
...quasdam pueris habebit ex omnibus fundis extra cameram et man cintarem...
...Alheydis p istum modum suis pueris...de ehidel matre ipsorum alheyds quitum de paterna
hereditate ipsorum penitus diuisa et sep...

Hermannus holscorp emit a katherina uxor hinrici stoynenuiz suas bodus...
...in erbuscheden sub suo cecto...

Katherina uxor hinrici stoynenuimes priscripta fecit hereditariam diuisione hinrici tuuckabel
suis pueris hermonie dietuzey in hunc modum ita q̃ dedit z assignauit suis pueris...
...p ipso hereditate paterna p quibus statuit dare...uuris stoynenuia suis pueris hinrici
tuuckabeli diuidente sue...in bledescode et suis pueris p istum modum de...
pueris suis de kieher...nec quem de paterna hereditate ipsorum penitus diuisa z separat

die weren·

Wer den andern beraubit sines
landes wider sinen willen ku

sin enis haut·

Wer den andern beraubit sin
ern an siner hanfvrauwen

36 In accordance with Saxon law, adulterers were buried alive and impaled.
Miniature from the Zwickau book of town law, 1348. Stadt- und Kreisarchiv Zwickau

37 The home of a wrongdoer, who has kidnapped a woman, is destroyed by fellow citizens.
Miniature from the Zwickau book of town law, 1348. Stadt- und Kreisarchiv Zwickau

38 A woman takes an oath before the Graz town judge.
Painting by an unknown master, 'Picture of the Town Judge', 1478, detail. Stadtmuseum, Graz

39 The court has ordered a dispute to be settled by open combat, in which the woman's weapon is a stone wrapped in a cloth. In order to counterbalance the physical superiority of the male, limits are placed on his freedom of movement.
Miniature from Heinrich von Neustadt's *Appolonius von Tyrland*, southern German manuscript, post 1400, Chart. A 689. Forschungsbibliothek Gotha

40 In an outdoor open combat between man and woman, the woman, armed with sword and spear, obviously has the upper hand.
Miniature from Diebold Schilling, *Spiezer Bilder-Chronik*, 1485, plate 36. Municipal and University Library, Berne

Following pages

41 Joachim and Anne, the parents of Mary, Mother of God, are depicted in front of the town gate of Jerusalem, dressed in the fashion of fifteenth-century Halberstadt burghers.
Ambulatory window, 'Anne and Joachim before the Golden Gate', ca. 1420. Halberstadt Cathedral

42 Double image of Philip the Younger of Hanau-Münzenberg, with his wife Margret Weisskirchner, who came from a middle-class background.
Painting on lime wood by the Master of the House Book, 'Pair of Lovers', ca. 1480. Museen der Stadt Gotha

43 Joachim, the father of Mary, provides the young mother with food. Such representations of men from the holy family in scenes involving mother and child provide evidence of the changes in marital and family relations which took place in the late Middle Ages.
Painting by the Master of the Scots Altar, 'Birth of the Virgin', ca. 1470, detail. Benedictine Abbey of the Scots, Vienna

44 It is unusual for men, here presumably the husband and the doctor, under whom the midwife is working, to be depicted in birth scenes.
Miniature from Pseudo-Jaquemart, 'Birth of the Virgin', late fourteenth century, Ms. lat. 919, fol. 28. Bibliothèque Nationale, Paris

Do man zalt / als / ec hoptens Jar an dem ach
tenden tag der kindlen bestatt ein kampf an
der matten an der statt do nu des bischoffs unser
statt / und kampften ein man und ein frow mit
enandern / und lag die frow ob .

Sus in aduito
rium meum in
tende.

omine ad adiuuan
dum me festina.

45 Daily maternal care in a busy scene.
Painting by an unknown artist, 'The Holy Family', 1510/20.
Museum of Fine Arts, Budapest

46 Portrait of a young Italian woman.
Painting by Sebastiano Mainardi, 'Half-length Portrait of a Young
Woman', ca. 1500. Staatliches Lindenau Museum, Altenburg

47 Scenes from Roman history on a chest, such as was commonly
found in the houses of the upper stratum of the town population.
Picture on a chest by Nicolo Giolfino, ca. 1530. Staatliches
Lindenau Museum, Altenburg

48 The interior of the house of an Italian burgher: Mary is sitting
on a chest; to the left there is a lectern, to the right, in the alcove, a
bed.
Panel painting by Barnaba da Modena, 'The Annunciation', first
half of the fifteenth century, detail. Staatliches Lindenau Museum,
Altenburg

49 Typical cupboard from an urban household with crenelation and tracery.
Painting by the Master of Maria am Gestade, 'The Annunciation', ca. 1460, detail. Church of the Redemptorists Maria am Gestade, Vienna

50 The interior of this well-to-do burgher's house contains a chest and a majolica jug. By the side of a bench with tracery work, there are wooden-soled slippers with leather straps, in the foreground an open cash-box.
Painting by the Master of Maria am Gestade, 'The Annunciation', ca. 1460, detail. Church of the Redemptorists Maria am Gestade, Vienna

51 French town burghers at dinner. The illumination is based on the wedding feast at Cana. A maid is lifting one of the jugs. At the lower edge of the picture the poor are being fed.
Miniature by the Master of the Parament (workshop), late fourteenth century, Nouv. acq. lat. 3093. Bibliothèque Nationale, Paris

52 Interior of a bedchamber: a wide wooden bed with the obligatory wooden ledge, a footstool, a small wooden chest.
Miniature 'Consummation' from Aegidius Colonna, *The Trojan War*, in the version by Martinus Opifex, 1445/50, Hs. 2273, fol. 18 r. Österreichische Nationalbibliothek, Vienna

53 St. Dorothy is given a fashionable hairstyle, a delicate pearl chain, and elegant collar; the upper part of her dress is sewn with pearls.
Painting by the Master of the Rottal Epitaph, ca. 1500. Old Gallery of the Landesmuseum Joanneum, Graz

54 The women accompanying Mary are dressed in the style of the urban upper classes of the second half of the fifteenth century. Note the person in the centre, whose headdress is skilfully built up into a peaked shape.
Painting by the Master of the Scots Altar, 'Marriage of Mary', ca. 1470. Benedictine Abbey of the Scots, Vienna

55 This picture of Mary displays countless details of the interior of a prosperous burgher's house: the bed with side curtains, and in front of it a chest and table. The clothes are made of fine materials. Painting by the Master of the Eggelsberg Altar, 'Birth of the Virgin', 1481, detail. Schlossmuseum, Linz

56 The elegant clothes worn by Mary and Joseph are barely distinguishable from those of the kneeling king. This scene from the life of Mary has been set in the milieu of the urban upper stratum. Panel painting from the Lübeck Altar of Mary, ca. 1500, detail. Church of the Virgin Mary, Parchim

57 Burghers enjoy themselves while dancing and bathing in the countryside.
Picture for the month of May, from the manuscript HS 3085, fol. 4 r., ca. 1475. Österreichische Nationalbibliothek, Vienna

58 The duties of a wife included accompanying her husband when he had a tooth extracted.
Pen drawing from a manual of chess, Codex poet., 1467. Württembergische Landesbibliothek, Stuttgart

Aber ob sy wurt gewar
Vnd sies verswig so gar
Langt das sie jns seitte me
Vor scham jch mûß sagen hie
Von einer die tet der vnglich
Als jch hort wan jch
An dem bûch mit fant
es wart mir von sagen erkant
Ein bischafft wie ein frowe jren man dar
Zû broht das er ließ den sierden zan vß brechen

59 Treatment of a child with hydrocephalus.
Miniature from *Chirurgia*, by Gerard of Cremona, twelfth cen-
tury, Codex Series Nova 2641, book 2, fol. 17r. Österreichische
Nationalbibliothek, Vienna

For a thyng, sires, saufly dar I seye,
That freendes everych oother moot obeye,
If they wol longe holden compaignye.
Love wol nat been constreyned by maistrye.
Whan maistrie comth, the God of Love anon
Beteth his wynges, and farewel, he is gon!
Love is a thyng as any spirit free.
Wommen, of kynde, desiren libertee,
And nat to been constreyned as a thral;
And so doon men, if I sooth seyen shal.

Revealing remarks with regard to the changing relations between the sexes appear in Chaucer's *Clerk's Tale* of his *Canterbury Tales* concerning the Griselda motif. (The Griselda tale is a strong advocation of the domination of man in marriage.) Chaucer writes that it would be surprising if one would still find two or three Griseldas in one town who would willingly tolerate such torment.[47]

✳ The autobiographical writings of three women from the upper classes of medieval towns—Christine de Pisan, Helene Kottanerin, and Alessandra Macinghi degli Strozzi—tell of a very close relationship with their husbands. Christine de Pisan describes her husband, who was nine years her elder and died at an early age, as an extremely considerate man who, she says, never lied to her and supported her in all she did. Alessandra Macinghi degli Strozzi, too, in her letters, communicates to her sons nothing but respect for her husband, who died after thirteen years of marriage. Her second son fulfilled one of her greatest wishes when he called one of his legitimate sons Matteo, after the grandfather. Who were these women whose own hands have left us the very fullest accounts of their lives?

Christine de Pisan, born in Venice in 1364, was the daughter of the doctor and astrologist Tommaso di Benvenuto, an extremely successful citizen. He occupied the chair of medicine at the university of Bologna and was connected by marriage with the city-state of Venice.

The father followed a call from the French king Charles V (1364–1380) and moved, in December 1368, to Paris. Christine was more thirsty for knowledge than her two younger brothers and, as she became older, made good use of the better opportunities for education offered to her by her new surroundings. She learned French and Latin, arithmetic and geometry; and librarian Gilles Malet gave her access to the treasures he had in his care.

At the age of fifteen Christine was married to the royal secretary Etienne du Castel, thereby joining the ranks of those women from the upper strata of town society who were linked to the royal court. She bears witness to the way in which individual women were able, through such links, to play a very active role in the social life of their time beyond the boundaries of their town. The early death of her husband left Christine not only in great despair but also in considerable financial difficulties. She began to write in order to lessen her grief. She also had, because of her precarious financial situation, to educate her children Marie and Jean herself. She wrote for them the 'Book of Wisdom' (*Livre de Prudence à l'enseignement de bien vivre*). Her following book, 'The Epistle of Othea' (*L'Epistre d'Othéa*), on the advice of a friend, she managed to sell to the Duke of Burgundy, Philip the Bold, for a considerable sum of money. Against all odds she became known as a writer and won much interest for her books. She dealt in them with important contemporary issues, as in her 'Book of Peace' (*Livre de la Paix*) and the 'Book of the City of the Ladies' (*La cité des dames*), in which she joined the debate about women's capabilities and criticised the attitude that regarded women as inferior. In the 'Book of the Three Virtues' (*Livre des Trois Vertus*) she drew up, from the point of view of her own social environment, a concept of education for women of all social ranks; in her own social milieu she was in favour of thorough education for women.

Helene Kottanerin, widow of the *Bürgermeister* of Ödenburg, Peter Székeles, who then married the gentleman-in-waiting of the provost of St. Stephen's Cathedral, Vienna, became lady-in-waiting of the queen consort of King Albert II (1438–1439). On the sudden death of the Habsburg monarch in 1439 the aristocracy in Hungary and Bohemia were concerned to find their own candidate for the throne, and rejected the idea of the infant Habsburg prince Ladislas Posthumus's succeeding to the throne. The king's widow, Elizabeth, approached her lady-in-waiting with an extraordinary request: Helene was to steal the throne insignia for Elizabeth's son Ladislas, who had been born after the death of his father. The barely three months' old boy would thus have a better chance of successfully pursuing his claim to the throne against the rival candidate put forward by the Hungarian aristocracy, Wladyslaw of Poland. The coup was successful and, for a brief period raised the hopes of success of the Habsburgs. However, these were soon dashed by the death of the queen.

In contrast to the rich variety of writings created by Christine de Pisan, the autobiography of Helene Kottanerin is concerned mainly with political affairs and her own role as lady-in-waiting and confidante of the queen. From the point of view of the social role of patrician women her account of the birth of Ladislas is of interest. The queen chose as assistants two honest widows from Ofen. They brought with them a midwife and another woman from Ofen, who was to be the child's nurse and had brought along her own baby. But Helene Kottanerin makes it quite clear that she herself was in a position to assist the queen. Widows from the town aristocracy were at times used fairly peremptorily. Thus the child Ladislas was put up in the house of the widow of an Ödenburg citizen without notice, and the owner had to leave her home without being able to take any of her possessions with her. It was only when the son-in-law of the widow concerned protested that Elizabeth ordered that she be offered appropriate lodging in the house of an Ödenburg patrician.

The third of the three women we have mentioned, Alessandra Macinghi degli Strozzi, was born into a merchant family in Florence in 1406. At the age of sixteen she was married to Matteo Strozzi. Her husband, who held important offices in the city, was sent into banishment during the political upheavals between 1433 and 1434 which finally resulted in Cosimo de' Medici coming to power. His wife followed him with their seven children. In the two years before her husband's death she lost three of them. In 1436, now a widow, but once more pregnant, she returned with two boys and two girls to Florence. When the two boys came of age they too were subject to banishment. Only the youngest son, born after the death of his father, remained with his mother and two sisters for some time after he, too, had come of age; then the eldest of the sons, who lived in Naples, required him to join him to support him and to be trained in the family business. It is because of this splitting up of the family that posterity has been left 72 letters from Alessandra from the years 1447 to 1469. These give an excellent insight into the everyday life of this woman who, finding herself in an unusual situation, used all her resources, wisdom, ingenuity, and determination to do the best by her family, not hiding her own suffering but bravely coming to terms with it and devoting her entire energies to those closest to her. She endeavours, by reducing her own needs to a modest level, and through skillful management of her tax affairs and occasional business deals, to retain what is left of the family fortune in Florence and make a new start abroad easier for her sons. She carries out complicated negotiations for the marriage of her daughters and keeps an eye open for suitable apprentices for her sons' businesses. When appropriate she writes advice to her sons, produces linen, towels, shirts, and fashionable collars for them at home, and sends them delicacies. At the same time she follows political developments in Florence and establishes contacts with influential people in the town council whose names, however, are only mentioned in code in her letters. Among other things she gives a lecture to the second son who is taking a rather unserious attitude toward his apprenticeship in Bruges, and refuses to answer to his extravagant needs. Above all, wishing to have grandchildren, she urges her sons to marry. On the other hand she displays tolerance of their illegitimate adventures with house slaves and makes arrangements for their offspring to be cared for. In one letter to her eldest son, Filippo, she writes, exasperated by his constant plans for marriage which never come to fruition: 'I pray God that he should free you from your fears, for if all men were so afraid of marriage as you are, the world would long since have died out! This is why we must help you to realise that the devil is not as black as he is made out to be, and must release you from your fears'. When her eldest finally does marry and the fifteen-year-old daughter-in-law is living under her roof, Alessandra proves to be an understanding support for the young woman and a faithful companion in her subsequent pregnancies. As is usual in upper-class urban families, the baby is given to nurses (either in the home or outside it) who are carefully chosen from women from the surrounding countryside. Once the child has been weaned it comes under the care of the grandmother, for the young, by no means robust mother is already expecting the next child. In connection with the extra work involved in her daughter-in-law's second pregnancy Alessandra writes: 'If I had no other interruptions in my work than Alfonso [the grandchild] that would be more than enough, but I have much pleasure from it; he follows me everywhere like a chicken following a hen'.

For all her sterling qualities Alessandra is every bit a lady of the wealthy town burghers. This does not emerge in her attitude to the slaves working in her own household. Toward them, with their close access to what is going on in the family, she displays a certain reserve, lest they betray something about the household, especially the marriageability of the daughters! Care is not displayed in her dealings with the poor tenants on her country properties. Thus she writes, in 1465: 'Piero and Mona Cilio are still alive, but they are both very sickly. I have leased out the property for next year, for I am concerned that it should be kept in good condition.

And if the two old people do not die, they will have to go begging. May God care for them'.[48]

✳ Alessandra Macinghi's correspondence, which reveals so much about her relationship with her children, prompts us to ask whether what she wrote is of general validity. Historical sources—lives of saints, court records, wills, letters, and chronicles—give us only chance impressions. What is clear, however, is that children, even those in the urban upper strata, were not always as well off as those of the younger Strozzi generation, who grew up in a relatively small family. Often—particularly in the households of the urban upper strata—a large number of children from various marriages of the father (more rarely of the mother) lived together. Even illegiti-

Woman bathing a child.
Woodcut, printed by Heinrich Laufenberg, Augsburg, 1491. In: Albert Schramm, *Der Bilderschmuck der Frühdrucke*. Vol. XXIII. Leipzig, 1943, ill. 382.

A woman helps a child learn to walk with a special apparatus. Such three-wheeled apparatuses were widespread elsewhere—for example, in Poland.
Woodcut, printed by Heinrich Laufenberg, Augsburg, 1491. In: Albert Schramm, *Der Bilderschmuck der Frühdrucke.* Vol. XXIII. Leipzig, 1943, ill. 385.

Thus, the chances of a close bond between mother and child evaporated. Or, circumstances changed through the early death of the father and remarriage of the mother. The stepfather demanded much attention for himself, his business, and possibly his own children whom he brought with him into the marriage, so that the mother had little time for an individual child. At best this role was taken by older brothers or sisters, close relatives or tutors. Johannes Butzbach reports of his own childhood: '. . .When my mother became pregnant again and was expecting my sister Margarete, I was taken from her breast at the age of nine months. My aunt, who was childless, took me as her child, and brought me up for many years with great tenderness and love until her death'.[49] His was by no means an isolated case. Nevertheless, a child often had a close relationship with its mother. Many wills testify to a close concern of sons for their mothers. The late age at which men married was to the advantage of mother-son relationships. In 1421, the mother of Henneke Behr, who had been gruesomely executed in Stralsund, persuaded Duke Magnus of Saxe-Lauenburg to gain the Stralsund council's permission for her to take down her son's body from the wheel and bury it.

In wills from the towns of the Hanseatic League the aunt on the mother's side *(matertera)* is often given special consideration. Thus the 1346 will of a male citizen of Stralsund makes provision only for his sister, his aunt, and the latter's two children. The daughter receives a mark and two cushions, the son a mark and a chest, the aunt linen, a mark, and the money for a pilgrimage to Aachen. The writer of the will thus gives her an important task to carry out for his soul, and allows her to request the necessary finances for this. In another Stralsund will the aunt receives a fur—elsewhere the fee for a nurse—and her sister one good and one old skirt.

Growing up in a town family did not, on the whole, spoil the children, and it gave them an early appreciation of the realities of life. When the childless wife of a rich Italian merchant from Prato, Francesco Datini, takes in

mate offspring of the husband—as often as not dating from a long period of bachelorhood before marriage—formed part of the household. In Italy their mothers were often household slaves, in northern countries, maids and housekeepers. In such large families, where infants were usually given to a nurse for the first two years of their lives, and boys started school or an apprenticeship in a merchant family (relatives or friends) when they were six or seven, an individual child often went without the close attention of its mother. She had often married young and was physically not in a position to care for her children intensively. Not infrequently, she died early, in childbirth or from sheer physical exhaustion, and was succeeded by a very young wife.

Parents are encouraged to bring up their children strictly.
Woodcut by an unknown master, 'The Bad Upbringing'. In: Johann Schwartzenberg, *Memorial der Tugend.* Augsburg, 1535.

Wer jungen kinder spart dj růt/
    Der leben findt man selten gůt.
Wann alter hund zů aller frist/
    Nit pändig recht zemachen ist.
Drůmb wölt jr kinder haben eer/
    Bey zeit gewent sy gütter ler.
Pflegt jr mit zucht vnd rechter trew/
    Deß hj vnd dort gewint jr rew.
Wer päsen kinden waich erscheint/
    Der ist jr aller gröster feint/
Vnd lacht yetzt deß jr nachmals greint.

her seven-year-old niece for a long period, the child's father writes: 'I am pleased that Tina wishes to read. I would ask you to put her right and punish her, for I think that she needs this'.[50] In addition to the girl Tina, in the Datini household there is the child of a household slave, who receives a careful education and eventually a good marriage. Italian moralists, like Paolo da Certaldo, tell parents to teach their daughters all the household skills—baking of bread, cleaning of poultry, sieving of flour, cooking and washing, making beds, spinning and weaving, embroidering silk, making linen and wool clothing, and darning stockings.[51] These were no empty demands; in the twelfth century, ten-year-old Bona from Pisa was selling her own spun silk at the appropriate price on the market.

In the middle and lower strata of town society, where the mother had to feed the infant herself, the mother-child bond was a close one, but the physical vulnerability of both was probably greater. Families such as that of Saint Catherine of Siena, who was the twenty-fourth child of a dyer, were not the norm, but the social position of such families forced the mother to be on a constant lookout for additional ways of earning money. One possibility was to offer her services as a nurse. The terrible circumstances that sometimes lay behind such transactions are suggested in a letter from the wife of the above-mentioned merchant Francesco Datini, who sometimes helped friends and customers find nurses. She writes: 'They seem to have disappeared from the face of the earth, for I can find none. And some whom I used to have, whose own children were near to death, now say that they are well. . . . I found one whose milk is now two months old. She has promised me that if her child, who is near to death, dies tonight she will come as soon as it has been buried'.[52] Above all, in poorer families, childhood ended at the age of four or five, when a child had to start looking after its younger brothers or sisters, help with the spinning, look after geese for payment, and help out in the household, garden, and vineyards. If the child did not carry out its

tasks properly the mother could be summoned before the town court to answer for it.

✳ If we try to gain an overview of the position of female town dwellers under law, in marriage, and in the family from the second half of the eleventh to the second half of the fifteenth centuries, what stands out compared with earlier times are significant changes in marriage and

Woman dressed in the costume of Basle.
Engraving by Hans Holbein the Younger. In: Georg Hirth, *Kulturgeschichtliches Bilderbuch aus vier Jahrhunderten.* Vol. I. Munich, 1923.

family law. But records of town laws do not always reflect these changes. The Catholic church's demand for marriage to be based on consent of the two people concerned largely benefitted the less well-off and the poor inhabitants of the towns, as it was their employers who insisted on the right to give permission for marriages, after they had freed themselves from their feudal lords where this restriction was concerned. For the children of the upper classes and the middle bourgeoisie the statutes relating to disinheritance constituted a severe restriction of their right to marry as they liked. They were still largely at the mercy of the marriage conventions of their social surroundings. Sometimes they attempted to avoid these restrictions through secret marriages.

For most female town dwellers what was of great significance, particularly in view of the very young age at which many married, were the changes in family inheritance law. The portion of the inheritance which was dependent on growth of the family fortune—usually a third but sometimes half, or even two-thirds—which the wife now received in addition to her dowry, raised her interest in her husband's financial affairs, and any work she did in the family business was rewarded. In cases where the husband was dependent on his wife's contribution, particularly in the case of craftsmen, the will often gave the wife access to the complete fortune.

One severe restriction for a woman with a large family was the reduction of her inheritance to the level of the children if she remarried after her husband's death. For the children's care and education, distribution of the inheritance had definite positive effects given the risk that remarriage could represent. It also forced marriage partners to give careful thought to their actions, and encouraged marriage based on genuine partnership and love. One aspect of the changes that occurred in the law in the late Middle Ages was the liberalisation of the guardianship of the husband over his wife. In many European large and medium-sized towns the wife received, during her husband's lifetime, the right of disposal of part of the family fortune (dowry, *Morgengabe*,

property transferred by the husband, annuities, inheritance from parents, brothers or sisters, or other relatives, bequests transferred during lifetime), although seldom over the entire fortune. She was able to dispose of these freely in her own will. Upper-class ladies also acquired property, houses, rents, and even fiefs, or they invested their cash in loans to the town or in businesses. In middle-class families the women now had the means to operate independently as shopkeepers, carry out business transactions, operate with small sums of money on the town bond market, build up their daughters' trousseaux or supplement the travel money of sons who were at school or serving an apprenticeship. In this way the position of married women was no longer different from that of widows or unmarried ones, although the latter were forced to have greater economic independence and, as a result of their rights and duties as citizens in their own right, were more closely concerned with the problems and affairs of the trades and crafts guilds and the town.

Hand in hand with women's partnership in property matters and the loosening of their husbands' power to speak and act on their behalf went an increasing recognition of their ability to take an active role in legal affairs. This applied, for example, to their involvement as parties to contracts, as executors of wills, as guardians, and as witnesses. Biographical accounts by urban upper-class women—we have seen portions of Alessandra Macinghi degli Strozzi's—demonstrate the extent to which a well-educated and experienced woman could play a central role in a family with very varied needs and demands.

It goes without saying that this progress in marital and family law hardly benefitted young wives who were exhausted by the birth of one child after another and the demands made on them by a large household with many children. And for the poorer families without citizens' rights the situation was obviously also different. In these circles the age at which girls married was probably higher. There was not the intellectual separation between husband and wife that existed in patrician families as a result of the difference in age and level of education of the two. Shared responsibility for children and household among the lower classes rendered the husband's naturally predominant position less obvious.

Despite the positive changes that occurred for the majority of female citizens and ordinary town dwellers as regards their legal position, the guardianship of husbands remained as a principle that could be invoked to regain rights already ceded. This situation remained, although the economic and social interests of the town burghers were pointing in another direction. This can partly be explained by the deeply rooted legal tradition and the tendency for the urban upper strata to imitate the life-style of the aristocracy as manifested in their emphasis, in marriage matters, on the importance of maintaining lineage. But in order to delve further into the complex reasons for this apparent paradox we will now look at the religious justification for the predominant position of the husband.

Religion
and Religiousness

The female town dweller's role in marriage, the family, the guild, and the community was determined not only by prevailing economic and social relations but by religious belief and custom. In Christianity, early attitudes toward women were inconsistent. Throughout the persecution, Christianity relied to a considerable extent on women's support; in the New Testament, Christ treats male and female members of the ancient Christian communities with a certain degree of equality. The Gospels record certain aspects of his behaviour which must have contravened then-current patriarchal practice and which were thus initially misunderstood by the disciples; we have, for example, the condemnation of the arbitrary repudiation of the wife by the husband (Matthew 19.1–19.11, Mark 10.1–10.12); the salvation of the adultress (John 8.1–8.11); allowing a woman to anoint the body or feet, a right that was usually performed by the man of the house (Matthew 26.6–26.13, Mark 14.3–14.9, John 12.1–12.8, Luke 7.36–7.50); and the treatment of woman as a conversation partner in her own right, as in the report in John of the conversion of the Samaritans (John 4.5–4.41). All the disciples mention Jesus' numerous female supporters (Matthew 27.55, Luke 8.2f., 23.55, 24.10f., Mark 15.40f.), and the active role played by female members of the community is well documented for the first three centuries A.D. The names of Saint Mary Magdalene, Junia, Saint Priscilla, and Paul's pupil Saint Thecla have been passed down to us as important female personalities in the early Christian communities. Thus we have the beginnings of a tradition that was to have a very positive effect on the shaping of the Christian image of the female, a tradition that could later be revived.

In the fourth and fifth centuries, an important phase in the development of the ruling Catholic theology—the religious doctrine which was to dominate the whole of the Middle Ages, and the period in which Christianity was being transformed from a religion of the persecuted into a state religion—the elements within Christianity sympathetic to women gradually disappeared. According to St. Paul (Corinthians 1, 11.5), women could make prophetic statements to the community only when wearing a veil, and they were thus forced into remaining anonymous. The picture of the two sexes propagated by the early Church fathers was influenced by neo-Platonism and was of great significance for the image of woman projected by the Catholic church. It equated women with sensuality, the body, the imperfect, and the transitory, and men with the soul striving to reach God. Since women were guilty of original sin and of continual attempts to dominate man's soul, they were considered to be sinful and inferior beings.

The equality of man and woman (Matthew 19.4ff., Mark 10.6ff.), deriving from the story of creation (Genesis 1.26–1.28), was substituted for a feminine elitist picture based on the ascetic ideal of lifelong virginity. The theologians of the fourth and fifth centuries were unanimous in their demand that the majority of women be submissive and obedient in all matters, man being the 'head' of the woman. This demand was based

The snake with a woman's head is a symbol of
woman's sinful nature.
Representation of the Fall of Man from *Biblia
Pauperum, Codex Vindobonensis* 1198, fol. 3 r.,
detail. Österreichische Nationalbibliothek, Vienna

on the claim that woman derives from man—which
again runs contrary to the first report of creation and the
corresponding passages from Matthew and Mark—and
that woman, unlike man, is not made in the image of
God and that Eve, when she seduced Adam, brought sin
into the world. Christian women were encouraged to
live in awareness of original sin, and men not to let themselves get entangled in the sinfulness of women. Another
warning to men to beware of women stems from practical rather than theological considerations and is found
in the writings of Saint John Chrysostom dating from
the second half of the fourth century. Having expressed
undisguised regret at the loss of the greater freedom men
had in their relations with women in the pre-Christian
era, when they were still permitted to 'have two women
at the same time'[53] and could spurn a woman they no
longer loved without being accused of adultery, he goes
on to argue how difficult it is for the man to adhere to
the Christian commandments, due to domestic cares,
the bustle of secular affairs and—in the worst cases—a
nasty, bitter, or difficult wife.

Both St. Augustine (A.D. 354–430) and St. Jerome
(ca. 347–ca. 420) advise Christian wives to lead an ascetic life. Augustine, however, who had a particularly
strong influence on medieval theology, handles with extraordinary sensitivity in *The Marriage Estate* the question of marriage for the purpose of producing offspring,
and of discouraging promiscuous sexual activity. He
even concedes that, according to the Bible (Corinthians
1, 7.4 ff.), woman like man has the right 'to the body of
the marriage partner and to be the active partner in the
relationship and vice versa'.

✳ In the time of the development of the medieval towns
the theological understanding of relations between the
sexes was already firmly established, and it was not particularly favourable to women. The writings of indi-
viduals who voiced somewhat less unfavourable com-
ments on women did not have any long-lasting effect.
These included the letters of scholastic philosopher and

theologian Peter Abelard to Heloise (his lover and the mother of his son, Astrolabus; as a consequence of her affair with Abelard, Heloise entered a convent and became abbess of Paraklet), which mention numerous positive female figures from the Bible. Such a less-prejudiced attitude toward woman can also be found in the works of Hugh of St. Victor (1096–1141) and Peter Lombard (ca. 1100–1160), both of whom emphasise partnership in marriage. The reasoning of Peter Lombard in this matter is particularly interesting. According to him God did not create woman from Adam's head, because she was not to be his ruler, nor from his foot, because she was not to be his slave, but from his side, because she was to be his companion and friend. Peter Abelard and Saint Hildegard (1098–1179) differ from the majority of their contemporaries, who had extremely conservative attitudes toward relations between the sexes, partly because they do not assess the human being's sexual behaviour in a completely negative manner but regard it as a biological necessity, vital for the reproduction of the human race.

The most influential theologians of the thirteenth century, especially Saint Albertus Magnus (ca. 1200 to 1280) and Saint Thomas Aquinas (1225–1274), took up the negative statements made by the Church fathers on the nature of woman, and treat her as an inferior being in the spiritual, physical, and ethical sense. They, like the Church fathers before them, base woman's subordination on her origin as part of man's body, and her role in original sin. She is advised by them to be totally obedient and to conduct all business through men.[54]

This Catholic-theological schematisation remained valid for the medieval town of western and central Europe; the commune movement of the town burghers aimed at, and achieved, far-reaching socio-economic, legal, and political freedoms but not spiritual emancipation. The fact that the burghers before the late Middle Ages hardly made any effort to bring marriage jurisdiction within its sphere of influence proved to be particularly disadvantageous for the female town dweller. The

authority of the church was extensively recognized, but this church-legal systematisation, which began with Gratian's book of decrees in circa 1140, was derived 'on the whole from the negative statements of the patricians, which were used to justify the restrictions placed on women, rather than to champion their rights'.[55]

The low value attached to the female personality by theologians left its traces in other important ideological areas. In Italian and old French poetry we find verse dat-

The Holy Family on the return journey from Egypt are dressed in simple clothing, similar to that worn by the middle and lower strata of the town population.
Illustration from *Biblia Pauperum, Codex Vindobonensis* 1198, fol. 3 r. Österreichische Nationalbibliothek, Vienna

ing from early thirteenth century specifically designed to warn men against the wiles of women, and listing the negative aspects of the female character. The anonymous author of *Proverbia quae dicuntur super natura feminarum*, a long epistle on the evil and falsehood of women, draws inspiration from the animal kingdom:

> A stubborn horse is not to be ridden at festival times, but to be kept in its stable or used as a beast of burden. . . . One cannot hope to change the nature of the pig, the cat, nor to spin silk from wool. It is also a waste of effort to try and coax a woman with mild or with hard words. . . . The fox has several exits to his lair; if the hunter thinks he has it already trapped, the animal flees into one and out through another. So too do women have plenty of loopholes and tricks. . . . The wolf changes his coat in summer, but he never changes his evil character. A woman may sometimes act simple and pious like a nun, but when it suits her, she may give her fancy free reign. . . . The basilisk kills with his poisonous look; the lustful eye of a woman brings scandal to man and dries him out like hay. It is a mirror of the devil; woe be unto even the most religious man, who looks in it too often. . . . He who trusts a snake is a fool; yet the snake deceived Eve and was condemned to crawl over stones and thistles. No man should trust a woman, after she deceived Adam, for which reason she should be made to cover her head and forehead, in order to show her shame. Woman's love is no love, but only bitterness; it should rather be called a school for fools.[56]

Verse containing more or less open anti-female sentiment could also be found in France and Switzerland, for example in the work of Peire de Bussignac, Jean de Meung, and the Bernese Dominican monk Ulrich Boner.

Just how deeply embedded the dominant role of man is in the consciousness of the town population can be seen in the less-prejudiced fourteenth-century didactic literature for women. Even such an understanding husband as 'The Parisian Housekeeper' *(Le menagier de Paris)*, as he calls himself in his pamphlet on the training of a young wife, demands from his own wife the submissiveness almost of a dog. She has to carry out all his demands, whether they be important or not so important, reasonable or unreasonable, in unquestioning obedience. The pictorial arts of this time are likewise full of images showing the inferiority of woman and her sinful character. Finally, the degradation of women was aided in an ethical and moral sense by the expansion of prostitution, which was encouraged by the secular and spiritual nobility, individual citizens, and numerous town councils.[57]

* The convent offered women a seemingly alternative way of life within the framework of the Catholic church, since a completely ascetic life and the overcoming of her 'feminity' could make her position within the sex hierarchy more bearable. Entering a convent was in the twelfth and thirteenth centuries almost the only way in which to gain a certain degree—in some of the convents a high degree—of education; the German and Italian mystics Saint Hildegard, Saint Catherine of Siena, Christina Ebner, and Adelheid Langmann even managed to gain public recognition. This route was, however, open to a relatively small number of the total female population. In England in the middle of the fourteenth century, there were only 3,500 nuns. Of the 111 female

60 The woman riding on the back of the philosopher Aristotle is avenging herself cunningly for the separation from her lover. Detail from the Malter carpet, 'Aristotle and Phyllis', ca. 1310/20. Städtische Museen, Freiburg im Breisgau

61 Temptation of St. Justina by the devil dressed as a woman. Painting by Friedrich Pacher, end of fifteenth century. Parish Church St. Justina

62 Nuns from the Order of St. Clare are deep in meditation. Painting by Giovanni del Biondo, 'St. Jerome with the Lion and Three Adoring Nuns', ca. 1365, detail. Staatliches Lindenau Museum, Altenburg

Following pages

63 Depiction of a well-ordered convent. Miniature from Ms. Add. 39843, fol. 6 v., French, ca. 1300. British Museum, London

64 Representation of hell. Devils bring in members of all the social estates in horse-drawn carriages, carts, baskets, and by rope. Miniature by the Master of the Brussels Initial from Add. 29433, fol. 89, late fourteenth century. British Museum, London

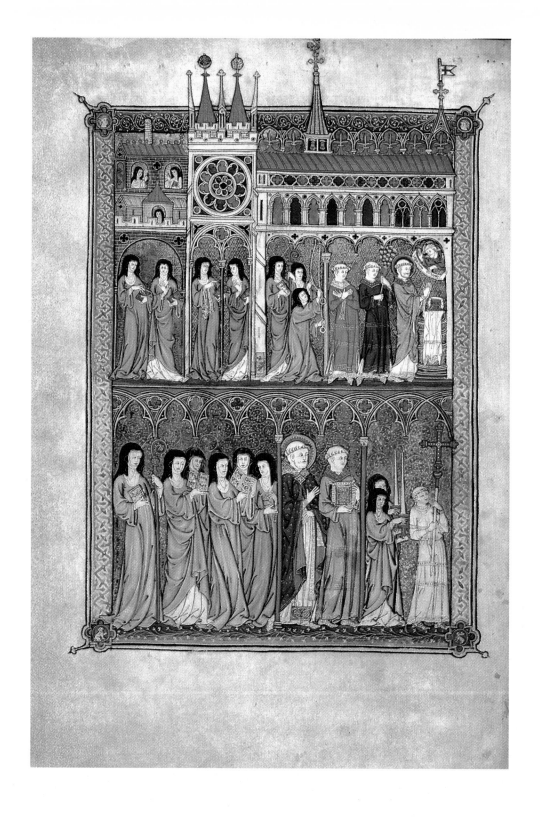

Dw ſold den durſtig trenkchn

65 Charitable deeds were part of the religious duties to be performed by the prosperous female town dwellers as well as by ladies of the nobility.
Miniature by the Master SH of 1485, 'Good Deeds', ca. 1500. Oberösterreichisches Landesmuseum, Linz

66 Scene from the life of Mary. To the left of the picture there is a representation of St. Catherine of Siena.
Panel painting by Sano di Pietro, 'Mary's Return from the Temple', ca. 1450. Staatliches Lindenau Museum, Altenburg

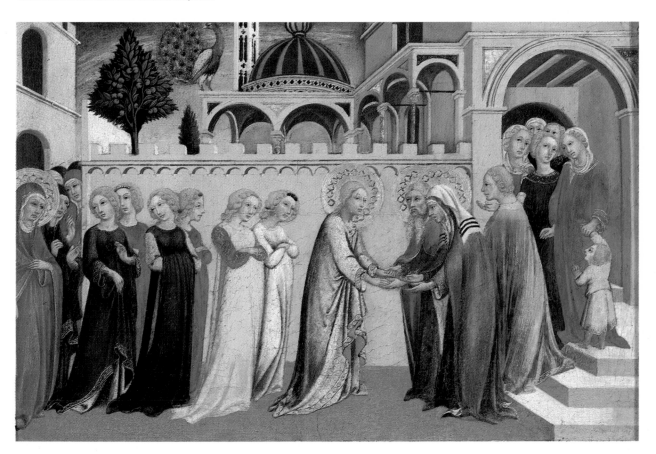

67 'Adoration of the Magi'.
Picture by an unknown artist from Lippova (?), 1510/20. Museum of Fine Arts, Budapest

68 'Mary and the Young Boy John Adore the Child Jesus'.
Panel painting by Pseudo-Pier Francesco Fiorentino, ca. 1460. Staatliches Lindenau Museum, Altenburg

69 The sculpture 'St. Anne with Mary and the Child Jesus' was part of the work commissioned by the successful merchant Hans Frenzel (1436–1526), who, when his wish he had made as a child was fulfilled, donated 8,500 Rhenish guilders for the foundation of a chapel.
Outside wall of the Chapel of St. Anne, Görlitz

70 Mary as the all-forgiving protectress is an image firmly embedded in the religiousness of the people. Representatives of all the social estates find shelter under her cloak.
Painting by an unknown artist, Upper Austria, ca. 1500. Stiftsgalerie, Kremsmünster

Following page

71 Owing to Renaissance influence, the representation of Eve indicates a reappraisal of this figure. Here, the over-proportionally large, majestic figure gives an impression of sovereignty and suggests that she is an important figure for the people situated to the left of the picture.
Fresco, 'Eve as the Mother of Mankind', Southern Tyrol, 1475/85. Filiale Church St. Nicolas, Klerant, Southern Tyrol

The devil on the long train suggests vanity and arrogance.
Woodcut, printed by Hans Vintler, Augsburg, 1486. In: Albert Schramm, *Der Bilderschmuck der Frühdrucke.* Vol. XXIII. Leipzig, 1943, ill. 705.

convents that existed in England in the late Middle Ages, 63 had fewer than 10 nuns in them.[58] In Germany there was a large influx into the convents in the twelfth and thirteenth centuries; the Dominican mendicant order alone had, apart from 49 monasteries, 63 convents in upper Germany. In the same area, numerous convents came under the Franciscan order. But if one bears in mind that they were not always positioned in the big town centres and that the number of nuns in any one convent could be quite small, one gets a more realistic picture of their modest scale.

Regulations prescribed strict seclusion for the majority of women in convents. The nuns of the order of St. Clare could receive a visitor once every fourteen days, but the presence of another respected sister was required and the conversationalists had to speak through a grill. Only once a year could the grill be re-

moved and the nun be seen by the outside world. The convents under the mendicant orders could not make, or improve, their living through begging. Since, however, the spiritual leaders of these orders were concerned to ensure that the convents remain economically solvent, the intake of women was manipulated in such a way that women from wealthy and generous families were admitted—i.e., families that could 'buy in' their daughter. The obligatory payment for admittance to the St. Clare convents throughout the whole of the southern German, Austrian, and Swiss area was an annuity of 3 marks or 40 pounds of pfennigs, which in the middle of the fourteenth century corresponded approximately to an income of 220 guilders.[59] Some less wealthy lay sisters could also be admitted; they acted as servants, performing various duties in order to allow the other nuns to enjoy prayer and contemplation. It was thus that most of the convents remained the reserve of the daughters of the nobility and the town patricians. From the twelfth and thirteenth centuries onward the nobility also sent its unmarried daughters and widows into semi-religious convents or religious communities which did not require the women to take vows or enforce strict rules with regard to seclusion.

* In a period that saw, on the one hand, the intensive development of the internal structures of their territories by the powerful feudal lords and the rapid expansion of trade and goods production, and on the other the retention by certain obstinate town lords of their traditional privileges, we find that there was understandably in the twelfth and thirteenth centuries movement and unrest among the people. In such circumstances, many were open to new religious doctrines. It was around this time that the heretic movement of the Cathari, the 'pure', gained ground in western Europe. These sects had their own centres from the end of the 1260s onward in the towns of northern Italy and southern France, and on the transport routes between these regions. Attempts to extend the movement to England failed. Men and women alike were allowed to make their way into the core of these sects; through strict adherence to all the doctrines they could become one of the 'perfect' (perfecti), who were regarded as the real bearers of the spirit. In comparison to the Catholic church the Cathari had a more positive attitude to women, through which they acquired numerous active supporters and sympathisers among the female town citizens. The duty of a 'perfect' was to lead an exemplary ascetic life in accordance with the Catharist doctrine—to disseminate and preach the basic ideas of the heresy. Women (perfectae) originally participated in the missionary work and preaching. However, once a spiritual hierarchy formed within the sects, women were excluded. There were no female Catharist deacons and bishops, but this did not lead to any significant reduction in the attraction of the sects among women—who

supported the basic principles of the Cathari: their demands for a poor church and the rejection of the Catholic church with its accumulation of wealth. Another group, the Waldenses, a pauper movement which was founded circa 1177 by the Lyon merchant Valdes, tended to attract women, particularly those of the middle and lower classes. Throughout the twelfth century it spread to southern France, northern Italy, and the area around Toul and Metz, until in the late Middle Ages it was a truly popular religion.

For the vast majority of female town citizens, however, the possibility of joining a sect was no real escape route. Only a few were willing to expose themselves to the dangers arising through the persecution of the heretic movement by the Catholic church. The crusade against the Cathari in southern France in 1209–1229 was a cruel example of this, and the persecution increased with the organisation of the papal inquisition in 1231. Certain elements of the Catharist doctrine, for example that of celibacy, and the rejection of procreation, probably served in the long run to alienate female citizens. In this respect their most fundamental interests were probably better represented by the Catholic church, which insisted on monogamy.

* In the early thirteenth century within the Catholic church there developed, with the mendicant orders of the Dominicans and the Franciscans, which we have already mentioned in another context, an institution tailored to meet the religious needs of the towns and destined to have a strong influence on the female population. The Franciscans, in particular, dealt in their preachings with the position of women and marital relations. Their close contact with the people put them in a position to identify and tackle important social evils, and often to hit the nail on the head, as did Bertold von Regensburg in his sermons on marriage in 1275. He refers to the town custom of marrying off girls of twelve to sixteen years to men who were in their prime or already on the brink of old age, which was based on the

assumption that young, untouched women were par-ticularly suited to bearing strong healthy children, and which caused permanent social damage in the life of the town. Many young women could not stand the physical strain of frequent childbearing and died early. The aver-age female life expectancy was thirty years. The children had to go without the care of mothers and often suffered psychologically as a result. Marital conflicts arose due to the difference in sexual maturity between man and wife, and these in turn led sometimes to criminal acts, but more frequently to lapses in Christian marital and sex-ual mores. Bertold von Regensburg, as a priest who heard confession, was well acquainted with the predict-able scenarios arising out of marriages between young girls and old men. Such unions supplied subject matter for many a medieval comic farce and were the impetus too for attempts undertaken by some town councils in the late Middle Ages to curb child abuse. Von Re-gensburg tackles this sorry state of affairs early on and without beating around the bush: 'I only want to advise you on one matter, which is not forbidden by God, but I bid you to take heed of my advice, which is given to you in good faith. Because we can see and hear the suf-fering caused by you giving young children to old men, I advise you to give a young maiden to a young man and an old one to an older man'. At another point he tackles the problem of unhappy marriages using question-and-answer form:

> Brother Bertold! But you say that the wife should be subordinate to the husband, and he should be her master. That is also correct, you should be her master and she your housewife; but this does not mean you should always pull her hair for no reason and beat her as often as you like, and curse and swear and mistreat her. You also should not wear good clothes and dress her in old rags; she should dress, eat, and drink in the same manner as you. For she has replaced God in your heart

and should therefore be dear to you. Anyone who does not care for his spouse in word and deed is far from the kingdom of heaven.[60]

It would be a mistake to conclude from these statements that a basic reorientation of Catholic theology with re-gard to the roles of the two sexes occurred in the late Middle Ages. Bertold von Regensburg and other the-ologians like him who were basically sympathetic to women's problems did not question the dominant role of the man in marriage, and indeed condemned any in-dependent attempts by women to improve their lot. What they were concerned with, on the whole, was the elimination of the most negative consequences of man's dominant role in marriage, which was discrediting the church-sanctioned marriage, and the spiritual leaders who advocated it. Experience had shown that this could lead to women turning away from the Catholic church, or to attempts to develop within the framework of the church new ways of life that were difficult for the au-thorities to control. The latter, however, happened de-spite their efforts to achieve the contrary.

✳ One obvious example of this is the Beguine move-ment, which gathered strength in the northern French and Rhenish area around 1200. The Beguines, like the Waldenses, were a section of the town pauper move-ment which was striving for a poor and purified church. These women, who came from all strata of the town population, united to form independent religious con-vents and lived according to rules set by themselves. Their common banner was the striving toward a virtu-ous life based on the ideal of poverty. The women guaranteed their material security through textile work, trade, care of the elderly and sick, by working as maids, performing funeral services, and by begging. Others lived from donations made by relatives or supporters. The Beguine convents came under the town jurisdiction and were organic members of the town community; some of their members had citizens' rights.

The Beguine phenomenon provided a religious way of life for women that was completely compatible with town life, and it thus spread quickly to Saxony, Thuringia, and Bohemia. It is reckoned that in the large European export towns, such as Ghent, Cologne, Basle, and Strasbourg, there were several hundred Beguines; we have concrete numbers for Mainz, which had 90 Beguines; Strasbourg, which had 160; and Cologne, which had 600. The latter were divided into approximately 60 Beguine homes. Even in the early thirteenth century the English monk and chronicler, Matthew Paris, expressed his astonishment at the large number of Beguines in Cologne. He writes: 'And their number grew in a short period of time to such an extent, that there were two thousand of them in the town of Cologne and in the surrounding area'.[61] As with other medieval chroniclers, the figures cited by Matthew Paris are exaggerated, but they do show that the Beguines in Cologne were a highly visible group. Average-sized trade and manufacturing towns such as Trier, Speyer, Ulm, Dortmund, and the maritime towns of Hamburg, Lübeck, and Bremen counted only a few dozen Beguines among their inhabitants.

The strong Beguine presence in some of the larger medieval towns bears witness to a striving among numerous unprovided-for female town dwellers, or among women who were anxious to avoid the male domination in marriage, to form alternative communities in order to lead a life that provided economic security without being overdominated by religious precepts. Beguines did not have to take strict vows, and house rules varied from convent to convent. Often the houses were so strongly allied with the textile trade that they represented serious competition for the guilds. One sentence pronounced by the Cologne council in a case involving emblem embroiderers and the Beguines

Thomas Aquinas meets a mystic, perhaps a Beguine. Woodcut, printed by Hans Vintler, Augsburg, 1486. In: Albert Schramm, *Der Bilderschmuck der Frühdrucke.* Vol. XXIII. Leipzig, 1943, ill. 665.

of the Schelen convent shows how serious these conflicts could be. It seems that in 1482, the emblem embroiderers forced their way into the Beguine convent in order to carry out a house search. This was duly condemned by the council as an act of violence, but the council nevertheless forbade the Beguines to carry on with emblem embroidery. In 1421 the Beguines of this convent had already been banned from the cotton-weaving trade, and were allowed to operate only six linen-weaving looms. Toward the end of the fifteenth century the Cologne Beguines were also subject to the ban placed on all spiritual institutions with regard to hat embroidery and beer brewing. A counterpart to the Beguine movement sprang up in the towns of the Netherlands and lower Germany in the form of communities of Sisters of the Common Life, founded by Geert Grote (1340 to 1384). They were also involved in textile production. In Deventer, where the movement began, it is reckoned that there were approximately 150 sisters at the beginning of the fifteenth century. In the same period there were about 700 living and working in Hertogenbos.

Within the Beguine movement, there were those who were heavily involved in the economic life of the towns, but there was also a smaller group of women who were born rich and could devote themselves to religious questions. In correspondence with the longings of large groups of the population their activities were aimed at the internalisation of their faith which had been discredited by the grievances within the Catholic church. The most famous of these were the German mystic Mechthild von Magdeburg who was, however, firmly entrenched in the Catholic church; the Englishwoman Margery Kempe; and Marguerite Porète, who wrote *The Mirror of the Simple Souls* and was burned at the stake in 1310 as a heretic. Such Beguines are also mentioned by the Franciscan Simon of Tournai when he writes, in 1273: 'We have among us women, who call themselves Beguines, some of whom are very sharp and open to new ideas. They have succeeded in translating the secrets of the holy word, which even people well ac-

quainted with the Bible find hard to decipher, into the French dialect'.[62] He adds that he himself had read and possessed a copy of such a Bible, which was on sale to the public in Paris bookshops, and denounces this translation as being full of heresy, errors, and doubts.

Marguerite Porète and the Beguines mentioned above were subject to close observation and persecution. The Catholic church opposed the Beguines because experience had shown that sections of the movement gave open support to the radical representatives of the pauper movement within the church, such as the Franciscan Spiritualists in southern France at the turn of the thirteenth and fourteenth centuries, who were uncompromising in their support of this ideal, attacking even the Pope. Moreover the Beguines who came from the poorer sections of town, lacked a secure social position, and were not attached to one particular convent proved to be highly susceptible to heretical doctrines such as 'free spiritual heresy'. They, like their male counterparts, the Beghards, who were also influenced by free spiritual heresy, were subject to persecution during the Inquisition. The majority of the Beguines, however, attached themselves to the Franciscan and Dominican mendicant orders, which were the orders closest to their ideals of a poor, purified church, and led a religious life while trying to avoid any direct confrontation with the church. Many originally Beguine convents seem to have been completely incorporated into the Franciscan orders and thus appear as the Third Order (Tertiaries) of the Franciscans. The Tertiaries were religious communities composed of women who led a religious life in the towns without taking vows, so that they could at any time leave the Order and devote themselves to the care of the elderly and sick. They are part of the numerous religious-cooperative associations that were formed by broad strata of the town population, and particularly by women, in the late Middle Ages. Another example of such a movement was the Kaland movement, which was widespread in Germany and was joined of both priests and laymen.

* Despite the relatively intense involvement of town women in the heretic movements of the Middle Ages, most female town dwellers, and in particular married women, remained within the orbit of the Catholic church. And judging from the wills and testimonies they left, their attachment to this institution was by no means halfhearted—one reason being that the church courts were willing to intervene in questions of marital law in their defence if the municipal court had refused support. More to the point, however, favourable de-

Stonemasons with a customer, who, judging by her clothing, comes from the upper stratum of the town population.
Miniature from the French novel of the Holy Grail, fol. 55 v., early fourteenth century. British Museum, London

The creation of Eve from Adam's rib. Of note are both the youthful appearance of God and the representation of Eve as Adam's equal, rather than a helpless female.
Illustration from *Biblia Pauperum, Codex Vindobonensis* 1198, fol. 3 r., detail. Österreichische Nationalbibliothek, Vienna

velopments in women's professional and economic situation gave them the self-confidence not to take too seriously the doctrine of the contemporary Catholic church with regard to man being the dominant sex. The idea was to manage to adapt the strict religious formula on how they should conduct their lives to their social circumstances. Both the wives of the town burghers and the economically independent women, as members of guild-type associations, saw that in order to enhance both their own social prestige and that of their family they must fulfill their religious duties conscientiously. We find in the wills of women from the prosperous burghers generous endowments being left not only to religious communities, churches, and priests but for the construction of churches, altars, hospitals, chaplaincies, and Beguine houses. At the same time we find pros-

perous female burghers embarking on long pilgrimages, possibly in part to satisfy their growing needs for broader education and experience. The Beguine Margery Kempe, mentioned above, travelled all over Europe. In Stralsund, several wills dating from the first half of the fourteenth century mention pilgrimages undertaken by female citizens. One of the most common destinations named is the Holy Virgin in Aachen. In the fourteenth century two women set off independent of each other from Görlitz to Rome. The Görlitz merchant Agnes Fingerin went all the way to Jerusalem on horseback, using country roads and sometimes in the company of nobility.

By the late Middle Ages many female town dwellers had, like Agnes Fingerin, adjusted their life aspirations to fit in with the Catholic faith. Hardly any of the secu-

With the consent of her heirs, the widow Anna Swelenburg from Mühlhausen leaves money for the building of an altar in the Bridge Convent.

Document no. 1114, Stadt- und Kreisarchiv, Mühlhausen/Thuringia

lar female town burghers would have thought to spend less on clothes as penance for Eve's original fall into sin. Wedding festivities were extremely extravagant, and the baptising of a child was an occasion for celebration, especially for the female relatives and acquaintances. Council decrees on the rules governing weddings, baptism, and clothes, as well as numerous moralising edicts, fought against these phenomena, but without any apparent success. The religious life of the late Middle Ages represents a synthesis of a religious attitude which was adapted to the everyday life of the majority of the town population and which was often very superficial, and a deep piety taken to its extreme by the mystics and the representatives of the pauper movement.

The position of women grew precarious with the introduction of the papal edict, or 'bull', *Summis desiderantes affectibus*, on the eve of the early bourgeois revolution in 1484, and in 1486 with the publication of the 'Witches' hammer' *(Malleus maleficarum)*, an infamous compendium for the introduction of inquisition proceedings against women suspected of being witches. This latter image persisted in all areas of life affected by ideology, although not all members of the clergy agreed to it.[63]

Outlook

The medieval towns as a whole witnessed a series of positive changes for all, including the female town dwellers. The extent of these changes varied according to the type of town, but they were the result of more favourable conditions, which allowed the town economy to flourish and facilitated the rise of the town burgher. Female inhabitants achieved a recognized position in the economic life of the town, limited legal competency[64], and the possibility to acquire the right of citizenship independently.

The women in the lower strata of town life in particular made a significant contribution to the family income by working and providing back-up for the family workshop, or by finding work outside the workshop, usually as wage labour and in small-scale trade. In the large manufacturing export and long-distance trading centres, as well as in the medium-sized trading towns exporting their manufactured goods, the small-scale female traders were undoubtedly one of the stalwarts of the internal market. In cases where the demand for labour exceeded supply, women from the lower strata of the towns often took on heavy physical work in construction or in smithies.[65] Many of these women also tried to earn on the side to improve the family income. The most vulnerable fell prey to prostitution.[66]

Women from the more wealthy town strata found work in trade, in currency exchange offices, in town offices and in craftwork. Despite the numerous limitations imposed by the guilds they could become masters, either in the exclusively female guilds, or in the mixed guilds of the textile trade. Other trades, such as oil pressers, rope makers, parchment makers, butchers, cobblers or bakers appear on occasion to have admitted individual female masters on a regionally limited basis.

Until the second half of the fifteenth century, in some cases to the end of the sixteenth century, there seems to have been a series of favourable conditions, encouraging independent female professional work, some of which disappeared in the early modern times. The main prerequisites for this were:

the geographical vicinity of home and the family business;[67]
the availability of cheap labour to help in the homes due to the relatively low demand for labour;
the interest of the town councils in providing the destitute women streaming into the towns with work, in order to lessen the burden on the town social services;[68]
the possibility of using the wife's professional activity to allow the man to devote himself to a town appointment;[69]
and not least the trend toward distribution in the leading export-manufacturing towns. (The combination of the husband working in trade and the woman doing the manufacturing, as in the Cologne silk trade, was typical of this trend.)[70]

The female town dwellers proved to be reliable family props in times of need, such as the death of the husband, demographic crises and conflicts within the towns. But also in normal town life, the efforts of the women served to secure and improve the family income, the social status of the family, the education of the children, the care and training of serving boys and maids, of apprentices, apprentice girls, unmarried journeymen and trade assistants, in that they lived in the house as part of the family.[71] Women were enabled to do so by participating to a certain degree in the commercial activity of the male members of the family, and in the daily events of town life. Moreover, the possibility of getting a primary education furthered their activity. Women from the numerically small upper stratum of the towns had already acquired a sound education mainly from private tutors. Long business journeys and pilgrimages broadened the horizons of some women. Their general cultural level, experience in medicinal, dietetic, and cosmetic matters, imposive life-style and impressive education meant that women from the town upper stratum in the late Middle Ages were in demand at the courts of the feudal nobility and as, we now know, allowed some of them to even express an opinion on public affairs. Christine de Pisan deserves a special mention, since she raised her voice publically in favour of political reforms that should help the French monarchy to reestablish peace in the country. For this committed person, who was acquainted with the Gospels as well as with the works of classical authors and of the Church fathers, peace was 'the epitome of all virtue, . . . the goal and the sum of all our efforts and work'. She acted in the conviction that 'without peace one cannot live with due propriety and moral fortitude'. Concerned with bringing peace to the kingdom of France, she tried, through such works as *Livre des Trois Vertus*, to influence her fellow women to act in this spirit. And in *Le Ditié de Jehanne d'Arc* (1429), following a temporary phase of resignation, she reaffirmed her militant philosophy, which was characterised by patriotism, staunch loyalty toward the French Crown, and a strong desire for peace. Christine de Pisan was also the first woman in medieval Europe to use her writings to protest against the degradation of her sex in literature and in the work of the school masters.[72]

As a preliminary summing-up, we can see from the above observations that the life of the female town dweller in the Middle Ages was not one long series of humiliations but included their active seizure of historical opportunities.[73]

Women's history has only recently been accepted as a discipline by the general body of historians, rather than being merely the research concern of individual historians. At present we only have a very sketchy idea of the life of women in the medieval towns. We can still not say anything definite on the scale of the changes for the better, and the extent to which they affected women from the various social strata. The extent and objectives of female activity on the town bond market, and the significance of female activity within the framework of the town economic and social structure have not been adequately explained. The same can be said of the reasons for the gradual retreat from the position gained by women in professional and economic life from the late fifteenth century onward, which is particularly notable at the end of the sixteenth century.[74] Many regional studies are necessary and many archives still have to be systematically searched, using new research methods. We can certainly expect an even greater differentiation with regard to time, place and type of the trends such as have been described here. On the other hand, a greater amount of local regional material will allow historical comparisons, which in turn will allow us to see more clearly sets of conditions underlying common trends. Those spiritual forces which acted as a forward-driving dynamism or as a brake must also be more clearly defined.

Questions with regard to the actual participation of merchant women in the life of the trade guilds[75] and the effect of those changes, positive for the female town dweller, on the women from the rural areas are as yet unanswered. The significance of the entry of women from the town upper stratum to the courts of the principalities[76]—as a result of the alliance of the influential town burghers with the local ruler in the late Middle Ages—still has to be evaluated. Another problem which has not yet been tackled is the relationship of the female town dweller to the medieval peace movements.[77] Likewise, the role of the Jewess in the European medieval town[78] has not yet been studied to any significant degree. If 'the full extent of women's influence on the form and movement of society is to be recognized',[79] one will have to delve deeper into the history of medieval women, in particular the questions raised here will have to be studied in all their multifarious aspects in separate branches of history.

Appendix

Notes

1 *Die Gesetze der Langobarden*. Ed. by
F. Beyerle. Weimar, 1947, p. 389.
2 Alpert von Metz, 'De diversitate temporum', in:
Monumenta Germaniae historica ss. IV, p. 719;
translated into German by K. Kroeschell, in:
Deutsche Rechtsgeschichte. Vol. 1. Hamburg,
1972, p. 121.
3 K. Kroeschell, *Deutsche Rechtsgeschichte*.
Vol. 1. Hamburg, 1972, p. 229.
4 *Ibid.*, p. 161.
5 E. Ennen, *Frauen im Mittelalter*. Munich, 1984,
p. 92 f.
6 'Chronik des Matthias von Neuenburg', in:
Die Geschichtsschreiber der deutschen Vorzeit.
2nd complete edition, vol. 84. Translated by
G. Grandaur. Leipzig, no date, p. 10.
7 Of the women concerned, 82.2 percent acted
independently, that is, not as part of a family
company. Cf. G. Jehel, 'Le rôle des femmes et du
milieu familial à Gênes dans les activités commerciales au cours de la première moitié du XIII⁰ siècle', in: *Revue d'histoire économique et sociale*
(1975) 2/3, pp. 193–215.
8 Cf. S. Rust'aveli, *The Man in the Panther's Skin*.
Old Georgian Epic. Translated into English by
M. S. Wardrop, 1912.
9 Document 1148 of the Stadt- und Kreisarchiv
Mühlhausen/Thuringia.

10 *Das Stadtbuch von Augsburg*. Ed. by
C. Meyer. Augsburg, 1872, p. 228 f.; *Das alte
Lübische Recht*. Ed. by J. F. Hach. Lübeck, 1839,
p. 291 f.; translated by P. Ketsch, in: *Frauen
im Mittelalter. Quellen und Materialien*.
Vol. 2. Düsseldorf, 1984, p. 182 f.
11 Quoted after E. Power, *Medieval Women*.
Cambridge, 1975, p. 61.
12 Quoted after *ibid.*, p. 62.
13 Quoted after *ibid.*, pp. 39–40.
14 P. Ketsch, *Frauen im Mittelalter. Quellen und
Materialien*. Vol. 1. Düsseldorf, 1983, p. 204.
15 M. Wensky, *Die Stellung der Frau in der
stadtkölnischen Wirtschaft im Spätmittelalter*.
Cologne, Vienna, 1980, p. 37 (= *Quellen und
Darstellungen zur Hansischen Geschichte*. New
series 26).
16 *Ibid.*, p. 61.
17 *Grut* is a type of wild rosemary that was used
for beer making until the mid-fifteenth century.
The word *gruten* came to refer to the whole
brewing process. *Grimms Deutsches Wörterbuch*
10, 2, 2. Leipzig, 1922.
18 *Quellen zur Geschichte des Kölner Handels und
Verkehrs im Mittelalter*. Ed. by B. Kuske. Vol. 1,
no. 652. Bonn, 1923, p. 223 f. (= *Publikationen der
Gesellschaft für Rheinische Geschichtskunde*.
Vol. 33, 1); translated by P. Ketsch, in: *Frauen
im Mittelalter. Quellen und Materialien*. Vol. 1.
Düsseldorf, 1983, p. 161 f.

[19] *Urkundenbuch der Stadt Heilbronn.* Rev. by M. von Rauch. 4 vols. Stuttgart, 1904–1922 (= *Württembergische Geschichtsquellen.*Vols. 5, 15, 19, 20). Vol. 3, no. 2084 b, p. 162 f.; translated by P. Ketsch, in: *Frauen im Mittelalter. Quellen und Materialien.* Vol. 1. Düsseldorf, 1983, p. 177 f.

[20] A useful collection of material is offered by P. Ketsch, *Frauen im Mittelalter. Quellen und Materialien.* Vol. 1. Düsseldorf, 1983, pp. 25 ff.

[21] Quoted after E. Power, *Medieval Women.* Cambridge, 1975, p. 68.

[22] Gerard of Cremona was one of the most important language scholars at the translators' school in Toledo. His *Chirurgia*, which appeared in the twelfth century, is the translation of the surgical tract of the work of the Arabo-Spanish physician, Abul Kasim, *Altasrif.* Complete facsimile version in the original format of Codex Series Nova 2641 of the Austrian National Library, Graz, 1979.

[23] Quoted after E. Power, *Medieval Women.* Cambridge, 1975, p. 86.

[24] *Die Chroniken der deutschen Städte vom 14. bis 16. Jahrhundert.* Ed. by the Historische Kommission bei der Bayerischen Akademie der Wissenschaften. III: *Die Chroniken der fränkischen Städte.* Vol. 4. Leipzig, 1862/74, p. 382 f.; translated by P. Ketsch, in: *Frauen im Mittelalter. Quellen und Materialien.* Vol. 2. Düsseldorf, 1984, p. 263.

[25] R. Alt, *Bilderatlas zur Schul- und Erziehungsgeschichte.* Vol. 1. Berlin, 1960, p. 198 f.

[26] Translated by P. Ketsch in: *Frauen im Mittelalter. Quellen und Materialien.* Vol. 1. Düsseldorf, 1983, no. 401, p. 256.

[27] Christine de Pisan, *The Book of the City of the Ladies.* Translated by Earl Jeffrey Richards. London, 1983, p. 85.

[28] *Urkundenbuch der Stadt Strassburg.* Rev. by A. Schulte and G. Wolfgram. Vol. 4.2. Strasbourg, 1888, p. 139.

[29] *Sachsenspiegel*, III, 45, para. 3.

[30] *Ibid.*, I, 31, para. 2.

[31] *Ibid.*, I, 45, para. 1.

[32] *Ibid.*, I, 45, para. 2.

[33] *Ibid.*, I, 24, para. 3.

[34] *Schwabenspiegel*, para. 26.

[35] *Ibid.*, para. 5a.

[36] *Ibid.*, para. 34.

[37] *Ibid.*, para. 76.

[38] *Sachsenspiegel*, III, 38, para. 2.

[39] *Ibid.*, III, 74.

[40] *Schwabenspiegel*, para. 21.

[41] M. Kleinbub, *Das Recht der Übertragung und Verpfändung von Liegenschaften in der Reichsstadt Ulm bis 1548.* Ulm, 1961, p. 88, A 552 (= *Forschungen zur Geschichte der Stadt Ulm.* Vol. 3).

[42] *Chroniken* A. 1, no. 2, fol. 68 v°, 69. Stadt- und Kreisarchiv Mühlhausen/Thuringia.

[43] *Wanderbüchlein des Johannes Butzbach genannt Piemontanus.* Ed. by L. Hoffmann. Berlin, no date, p. 158 f.

[44] *Das Mühlhäuser Reichsrechtsbuch.* Ed. by H. Mayer, 2nd ed. Weimar, 1934, p. 107.

[45] *Libri proscriptionum* II, fol. 73. Ratsarchiv Görlitz.

[46] *Urkundenbuch der Stadt Freiberg in Sachsen.* Ed. by H. Ermisch. Vol. 3, no. 674. Leipzig, 1891, p. 212 (= *Codex diplomaticus Saxoniae Regiae* 2, 14).

[47] F. N. Robinson, *The Works of Geoffrey Chaucer.* 2nd ed. London, 1957.

[48] Alessandra Macinghi degli Strozzi, *Lettere di una gentildonna fiorentina del sec. XV ai figliuoli esuli.* Ed. by C. Guasti. Florence, Sansoni, 1877; German translation: Macinghi degli Strozzi, Alessandra, *Briefe.* Edited and introduced by A. Doren. Jena, 1927 (= *Das Zeitalter der Renaissance* 1, 10), no. 72, p. 313, no. 62, p. 268.

[49] *Wanderbüchlein des Johannes Butzbach*

genannt Piemontanus. Ed. by L. Hoffmann.
Berlin, no date, pp. 9 ff.

[50] Quoted after James Bruce Ross, 'Das Bürger-
kind in den italienischen Stadtkulturen zwischen
dem vierzehnten und dem frühen sechzehnten Jahrhundert', in: *Hört ihr die Kinder weinen? Eine
psychogenetische Geschichte der Kindheit.* Ed. by
L. de Mause. Frankfurt on Main, 1979, p. 296.

[51] Quoted after *ibid.*, p. 295.

[52] Quoted after *ibid.*, p. 271.

[53] 'Johannes Chrysostomos über die von der Frau
ausgehenden Gefahren', in: P. Ketsch, *Frauen
im Mittelalter. Quellen und Materialien.* Vol. 2,
Düsseldorf, 1984, p. 48.

[54] E. Gössmann, *Die streitbaren Schwestern.
Was will die feministische Theologie?* Freiburg
im Breisgau, 1981, p. 84.

[55] *Ibid.*, p. 82.

[56] 'Proverbia quae dicuntur super natura
feminarum'. Translated into German and edited
by A. Tobler, in: *Zeitschrift für romanische
Philologie* (1885) IX, pp. 287 ff.

[57] The numerous penitent and Magdalene
convents founded in the thirteenth century to
give shelter to former prostitutes did not serve
this function for long. In the late Middle Ages
they became refuges for the unmarried daughters
of the patricians and of the nobility.

[58] E. Power, *Medieval Women.* Cambridge, 1975,
p. 89.

[59] Only 14 percent of the population of Basle was
taxed on an income of this size. Cf. V. Gerz von
Büren, *Geschichte des Clarissenklosters St. Clara
in Kleinbasel 1266–1529.* Basle, 1969, p. 57.

[60] *Die Predigten des Franziskaners Bertold von
Regensburg.* Translated and completely edited by
F. Göbel, 5th ed. Regensburg, 1929,
pp. 285 – 306.

[61] Excerpts from the greater chronicle of Matthew
Paris, translated into German by G. Grandaur and

W. Wattenbach, in: *Die Geschichtsschreiber der
deutschen Vorzeit 73.* Leipzig, 1896, p. 155.

[62] Warning given by the Franciscan friar Simon
of Tournai on the dangers of the Beguines, 1273,
in: H. Grundmann, *Religiöse Bewegungen im
Mittelalter. Untersuchungen über den geschichtlichen Zusammenhang zwischen Ketzerei,
den Bettelorden und der religiösen Frauen-
bewegung im 12./13. Jahrhundert und über die
Grundlagen der deutschen Mystik.* 3rd ed.
Darmstadt, 1970, p. 338; translated by P. Ketsch,
in: *Frauen im Mittelalter. Quellen und Materialien.* Vol. 2. Düsseldorf, 1984, p. 349.

[63] Among those who advocated greater respect for
women were Jean Gerson (1363–1429), Albrecht
von Eyb (1420–1475), the author of the 1452 *Apel-
latio mulieris Bambergensium*, and Agrippa von
Nettesheim. For more on the role of these three
men, see H. D. Heimann, 'Über Alltag und Anse-
hen der Frau im späten Mittelalter—oder: Vom
Lob der Frau im Angesicht der Hexe', in: *Frau im
spätmittelalterlichen Alltag. Internationaler Kongress, Krems an der Donau 2. bis 5. Oktober 1984,
Sitzungsberichte der Österreichischen Akademie
der Wissenschaften, Philologisch-historische
Klasse.* Vol. 473. Vienna, 1986 (= *Veröffentlichungen des Instituts für Mittelalterliche Realienkunde Österreichs.* No. 9), pp. 271 ff.

[64] G. Kocher points out the strong regional differences in the legal position of the medieval woman,
and also the legal advantages for unmarried
women. Cf. 'Die Frau im spätmittelalterlichen
Rechtsleben', in: *Ibid.*, p. 485 f.

[65] Women also participated in the building of the
Périgord college in Toulouse 1365–1371; almost
half of those who worked on the construction were
women. They transported stones and tiles, helped
demolish walls and dig out ditches. Their pay,
however, was well below that of the male workers.
Cf. J. Verdon, 'La vie quotidienne de la

femme en France au bas moyen âge', in:
Ibid., p. 365 f.

[66] In Dijon 50 percent of these women were forced into this form of existence because of violence (of these 27 percent were rape victims) and 25 percent were pressured into it by their families. Only 15 percent chose it more or less of their own free will. 'La misère qu'elle fût directe (ouvrières) ou indirecte (difficultés de réinsertion après viol, problèmes familiaux) constituait ainsi le principal facteur'. Cf. J. Verdon, 'La vie quotidienne de la femme en France au bas moyen âge', in: *Ibid.*, p. 370.

[67] Cf. E. Ennen, 'Die Frau in der mittelalterlichen Stadt', in: *Mensch und Umwelt im Mittelalter*. Ed. by B. Herrmann. Stuttgart, 1986, p. 47.

[68] For the extent and causes of female migration cf. M. Mitterauer, 'Familie und Arbeitsorganisation in städtischen Gesellschaften des späten Mittelalters und der frühen Neuzeit', in: *Haus und Familie in der spätmittelalterlichen Stadt*. Ed. by A. Haverkamp. Cologne, Vienna, 1984 (= *Städteforschung*. Series A, vol. 18), p. 18 f.

[69] M. Wensky claims that 'almost 30 percent of the registered female silk makers' had members of their family sitting in the town council. Cf. 'Die Frau in Handel und Gewerbe vom Mittelalter bis zur frühen Neuzeit', in: *Die Frau in der deutschen Wirtschaft*. Ed. by H. Pohl. Stuttgart, 1985 (= *Zeitschrift für Unternehmensgeschichte*. Vol. 35), p. 41.

[70] E. Ennen, 'Die Frau in der mittelalterlichen Stadt', in: *Mensch und Umwelt im Mittelalter*. Ed. by B. Herrmann. Stuttgart, 1986, p. 45 f.

[71] From the second half of the fourteenth century onward a journeyman movement can be detected in the European towns; in Germany it was stronger at the turn of the century (fourteenth/fifteenth). From this point onward one can no longer see the family as a 'family of the whole house'. Ac-cording to Knut Schulz, research has not yet come up with sufficient evidence to prove that journeymen were integrated in the house and family of the master craftsman even in the previous period. Cf. 'Die Stellung der Gesellen in der spätmittelalterlichen Stadt', in: *Haus und Familie in der spätmittelalterlichen Stadt*. Ed. by A. Haverkamp. Cologne, Vienna, 1984 (= *Städteforschung*. Series A, vol. 18), p. 315 f.

[72] Cf. *Le Livre de la paix of Christine de Pisan*. Ed. by C. C. Willard. The Hague, 1958; Christine de Pisan, *Le Ditié de Jehanne d'Arc*. Ed. by A. F. Kennedy and K. Varty. Oxford, 1978; Thomas Hoccleve, 'The Letter of Cupid', in: *Hoccleve's Minor Poems*. London, 1932.

[73] H. Wunder, who in a recent study goes into conceptional questions, and speaks out against the separation of women's history from the history of society, also criticises traditional research for reducing the history of women 'to the history of either their oppression or their emancipation'. Cf. 'Frauen in der Gesellschaft Mitteleuropas im späten Mittelalter und in der Frühen Neuzeit (15. bis 18. Jahrhundert)', in: *Hexen und Zauberer. Die grosse Verfolgung—ein europäisches Phänomen in der Steiermark*. Ed. by H. Valentinitsch. Graz, Vienna, 1987, p. 123.

[74] Further research possibilities are presented in the above cited essay by H. Wunder.

[75] Membership is made open to women for example in the statutes of the trade guilds of York (1430) and in the town law of the German town of Göttingen. Cf. C. Gross, *The guild merchant—a contribution to British municipal history*. Vol. 2, Oxford, 1890, p. 57; *Göttinger Statuten. Akten zur Geschichte der Verwaltung und des Gildewesens der Stadt Göttingen bis zum Ausgang des Mittelalters*. Rev. by G. Freiherr von der Ropp. Hanover, Leipzig, 1907 (= *Quellen und Darstellungen zur Geschichte Niedersachsens*.

Ed. by Historischer Verein für Niedersachsen. Vol. XXV), no. 264, p. 444.

[76] Cf. H. Ebner, 'Die soziale Stellung der Frau im spätmittelalterlichen Österreich', in: *Frau im spätmittelalterlichen Alltag*. Vienna, 1986, p. 536.

[77] In this connection we should mention the idea of peace propagated by the Tertiary, Catherine of Siena (1347–1379), who came from and worked in the milieu of the town burgher.

[78] This question has been tackled in recent works by E. Ennen and H. Ebner. Cf. E. Ennen, 'Die Frau in der mittelalterlichen Stadt', in: *Mensch und Umwelt im Mittelalter*. Ed. by B. Herrmann. Stuttgart, 1986, pp. 42ff.; H. Ebner, 'Die soziale Stellung der Frau im spätmittelalterlichen Österreich', in: *Frau im spätmittelalterlichen Alltag*. Vienna, 1986, pp. 529ff.

[79] This qualified task was formulated by W. Affeldt in 'Einführung. Frühmittelalter und historische Frauenforschung', in: *Interdisziplinäre Studien zur Geschichte der Frauen im Frühmittelalter. Methoden—Probleme—Ergebnisse*. Ed. by W. Affeldt and Annette Kuhn, Düsseldorf, 1986 (= *Frauen in der Geschichte*; 7/ *Geschichtsdidaktik: Studien, Materialien*. Vol. 39), p. 21.

Sources

Unpublished sources

Ratsarchiv Görlitz
*Bereit von Jüterbog's Annalen der Stadt Görlitz
    (1418–1419)*
Briefbücher (1487–1491)
Hans Brückners Krämerbuch
Magdeburger Schöppensprüche
Urkundenregesten des Ratsarchivs

Staatsarchiv Dresden
Schöffenbuch from Chemnitz
Memorialbuch from Lössnitz
Stadtbuch II from Mittweida

Stadtarchiv Erfurt
Liber causarum (1424–1435)
Stadtbuch (1482–1492) (private disputes)

Stadtarchiv Leipzig
Ratsbuch (1466–1489)

Stadt- und Kreisarchiv Mühlhausen/Thuringia
Bruchbücher (1460–1500)
Chronicon Mühlhusinum
Copialbücher (1382–1391)
Gerichtsbücher (1431f., 1437, 1447–1449)
Kämmereiregister (1418–1420)
Kataster (1400, 1414, 1470)
Notulbücher (1371f., 1415ff.–1444)
Urfehdebücher (1441ff.–1470)
Urkunden

Stadtarchiv Stralsund
Bruchstücke des alten Kataster
*Testamente (Regesten des Stadtarchivs Stralsund)
    (1416–1457)*
Das zweitälteste Bürgerbuch (1349–1571)

Stadt- und Kreisarchiv Zwickau
Amtsbücher (1503f., 1516–1521)
Konzeptbuch (1490f., 1506)
Liber Proscriptionum de anno 1367 ad annum 1536
Quittungen und Briefe (1401–1490)
Stadtbuch I–III
Testamente (15. Jahrhundert)

Published sources

*Die Acht-, Verbots- und Fehdebücher Nürnbergs von
    1285–1400.* Rev. by W. Schultheiss. Nuremberg,
    1959 (= *Nürnberger Rechtsquellen* 1–2).
Altdeutsches Decamerone. Ed. by W. Spiewok. Berlin,
    no date.
Das älteste Berliner Bürgerbuch 1453–1700. Ed. by
    P. Gebhardt. Berlin, 1927.
Das älteste Bürgerbuch der Stadt Soest 1302–1449. Ed.
    by H. Rothert. Münster, 1958 (= *Veröffentlichungen
    der Historischen Kommission für Westfalen* XXVII).
*Die ältesten Osnabrückischen Gildeurkunden (bis
    1500).* Ed by F. Philippi. Osnabrück, 1890.
Das älteste Stralsunder Bürgerbuch (1319–1348). Rev.
    by R. Ebeling. Stettin, 1926 (= *Veröffentlichungen
    der Historischen Kommission für Pommern*).
Das älteste Wismarsche Stadtbuch. Ed. by F. Techen.
    Wismar, 1912.
*Amtsbuch der Reichsstadt Nordhausen 1312–1345.
    Liber privilegiorum et album civium.* Ed. by
    W. Müller. Nordhausen, 1956.
Etienne Boileau, *Le livre des métiers. Les métiers
    et corporations de la ville de Paris.* Ed. by
    R. Lespinasse and F. Bonnardot. Paris, 1877.
A. von Brandt, *Regesten Lübecker Bürgertestamente.*
    Lübeck, 1973 (= *Veröffentlichungen zur Geschichte
    der Hansestadt Lübeck.* Vol. 24).
Die Chronik des Matthias von Neuenburg. Translated
    by G. Grandaur. Leipzig, no date (= *Die Geschichts-
    schreiber der deutschen Vorzeit.* 2nd complete ed.,
    vol. 84).

Die Chroniken der deutschen Städte vom 14. bis 16. Jahrhundert. Leipzig, 1862–1931.

Codex diplomaticus Lusatiae superioris II–VI. Görlitz, 1896–1931.

Colmarer Stadtrechte. Rev. by P. W. Finsterwalder. Heidelberg, 1938 (= *Oberrheinische Stadtrechte* III, 3).

Die Denkwürdigkeiten der Helene Kottanerin (1439 bis 1446). Ed. by K. Mollay. Vienna, 1972 (= *Wiener Neudrucke, Neuausgaben und Erstdrucke deutscher literarischer Texte.* Vol. 2).

B. Diestelkamp, 'Quellensammlung zur Frühgeschichte der deutschen Stadt (bis 1250)', in: *Elenchus fontium hist. urb. quem edendum curaverunt C. van de Kieft et J. E. Niermeyer.* Leiden, 1967.

'Frauenarbeit im Mittelalter. Quellen und Materialien'. Compilation and introduction by P. Ketsch, in: *Frauen im Mittelalter.* Ed. by A. Kuhn. Vol. 1. Düsseldorf, 1983.

'Frauenbild und Frauenrechte in Kirche und Gesellschaft. Quellen und Materialien'. Compilation and introduction by P. Ketsch, in: *Frauen im Mittelalter.* Ed. by A. Kuhn. Vol. 2, Düsseldorf, 1984.

Göttinger Statuten. Akten zur Geschichte der Verwaltung und des Gildewesens der Stadt Göttingen bis zum Ausgang des Mittelalters. Rev. by G. Freiherr von der Ropp. Hanover, Leipzig, 1907 (= *Quellen und Darstellungen zur Geschichte Niedersachsens.* Ed. by Historischer Verein für Niedersachsen. Vol. XXV).

Hamburgische Bursprachen 1346–1594 mit Nachträgen bis 1699. Rev. by J. Bolland. Parts 1 and 2. Hamburg, 1960 (= *Veröffentlichungen aus den Staatsarchiven der Freien und Hansestadt Hamburg.* Vol. VI)

Hamburgische Chroniken in niedersächsischer Sprache. Ed. by J. M. Lappenberg, Hamburg, 1861 (Reprint Niederwalluf, 1971).

Handel und Verkehr über die Bündner Pässe im Mittelalter zwischen Deutschland, der Schweiz und Oberitalien. Rev. by W. Schnyder. Vol. 1. Zurich, 1973.

F. Keutgen, *Urkunden zur städtischen Verfassungsgeschichte.* Berlin, 1899.

Das Konstanzer Leinengewerbe. Part 2: *Quellen.* Rev. by F. Wielandt. Constance, 1953 (= *Konstanzer Stadtrechtsquellen* III).

Die Leibdingbücher der Freien Reichsstadt Augsburg 1330–1500. Ed. by A. Haemmerle. Munich, 1958.

Le livre de Bourgeoisie de la ville de Strasbourg. Ed. by C. Wittmer and G. C. Meyer. Strasbourg, Zurich, 1948.

Le Menagier de Paris. Ed. by J. Pichon. Vol. 1. Paris, 1846.

Das Mühlhäuser Reichsrechtsbuch. Ed. by H. Mayer. Weimar, 1934.

Das Neue Testament. Revised after the translation by Martin Luther, revised text, 1975. Evangelische Haupt-Bibelgesellschaft zu Berlin und Altenburg, no date.

Nuovi Documenti del Commercio Veneto dei sec. XI–XIII. Ed. by A. Lombardo and R. Morazzo della Rocca. Venice, 1953 (= *Monumenti storici.* New series, vol. VII).

Die Nürnberger Bürgerbücher. Die Pergamentenen Neubürgerlisten 1302–1448. Ed. by Stadtarchiv Nürnberg. Nuremberg, 1974 (= *Quellen zur Geschichte und Kultur der Stadt Nürnberg.* Vol. 9).

Nürnberger Polizeiordnungen aus dem 13. bis 15. Jahrhundert. Ed. by K. Bader. Stuttgart, 1861 (= *Bibliothek des literarischen Vereins Stuttgart.* Vol. 62).

Nürnberger Totengeläutbücher I, St. Sebald 1439–1517. Rev. by H. Bürger. Neustadt, 1961.

Das Ofener Stadtrecht. Eine deutschsprachige Rechtssammlung des 15. Jahrhunderts. Ed. by K. Mollay. Weimar, 1959.

O. Pickl, *Das älteste Geschäftsbuch Österreichs. Die Gewölberegister der Wiener Neustädter Firma Alexius Funck (1516–1538) und verwandtes Material zur Geschichte des steirischen Handels im 15./16. Jahrhundert.* Graz, 1966 (= *Forschungen zur geschichtlichen Landeskunde der Steiermark.* Vol. 23).

O. Pickl, 'Innerösterreichische Handelsbeziehungen zu Süddeutschland und Venedig im Spiegel von Behaim-Handelsbriefen der Jahre 1418 bis 1457', in: *Festschrift für F. Hausmann*. Ed. by H. Ebner. Graz, 1977, pp. 379–408.

Christine de Pisan, *Le chemin de long estude*. Ed. by R. Püschel. Berlin, Paris, 1881.

Christine de Pisan, *Les épistres sur le roman de la rose*. Ed. by F. Beck. Neuberg, 1888.

Christine de Pisan, *Le livre de la paix*. Ed. by C. C. Willard. The Hague, 1958.

'Proverbia quae dicuntur super natura feminarum'. Ed. by A. Tobler, in: *Zeitschrift für romanische Philologie* (1885) IX, pp. 287–331.

S. Rust'aveli, *The Man in the Panther's Skin. Old Georgian Epic*. Translated into English by M. S. Wardrop, 1912.

Sanct-Ulrichs-Bruderschaft Augsburg: Mitglieds-Verzeichnis 1466–1521. Ed. by A. Haemmerle. Munich, 1949.

D. Schilling, *Spiezer Bilder-Chronik 1485*. Berne, 1939.

Schlettstadter Stadtrechte. Vol. 1. Rev. by J. Gény. Heidelberg, 1902 (= *Oberrheinische Stadtrechte* III, 1).

Schriftdenkmäler des steirischen Gewerbes. Rev. by F. Popelka. Graz, 1950.

Les statuts municipaux de Marseille. Ed. by R. Pernoud. Monaco, Paris, 1949.

O. Staudinger, 'Löbauer Urkunden-Regesten', in: *Löbauer Heimatblätter*. Annual sets 1933–1935, nos. 113–148.

Die Steuerbücher von Stadt und Landschaft Zürich des XIV. und XV. Jahrhunderts. Rev. by H. Nabholz and F. Hegi. Zurich, 1918.

Alessandra Macinghi degli Strozzi, *Briefe*. Ed. by A. Doren. Jena, 1927 (= *Das Zeitalter der Renaissance. Ausgewählte Quellen zur Geschichte der italienischen Kultur* 1, 10).

Überlinger Einwohnerbuch 1444–1800. Ed. by F. Harzendorf. Überlingen, 1968.

Ulmisches Urkundenbuch. Vol. 1. Ed. by F. Pressel. Stuttgart, 1873.

Urkundenbuch der ehemals freien Reichsstadt Mühlhausen in Thüringen. Rev. by K. Herquet. Halle, 1874.

Urkundenbuch der Stadt Bielefeld und des Stifts Bielefeld. Ed. by B. Vollmer. Bielefeld, Leipzig, 1937.

Urkundenbuch der Stadt Erfurt. Vol. 1. Rev. by C. Beyer. Halle, 1889 (= *Geschichtsquellen der Provinz Sachsen und angrenzender Gebiete*. Vol. 23).

Urkundenbuch der Stadt Esslingen. Rev. by A. Diehl. Vol. 1. Stuttgart, 1899 (= *Württembergische Geschichtsquellen*. Vol. 4).

Urkundenbuch der Stadt Freiberg in Sachsen. Ed. by H. Ermisch. Vol. 3. Leipzig, 1891 (= *Codex diplomaticus Saxoniae Regiae* 2, 14).

Urkundenbuch der Stadt Freiburg im Breisgau. Rev. by F. Hefele. Freiburg im Breisgau, 1940.

Urkundenbuch der Stadt Friedberg. Vol. 1 (1216–1410). Rev. by M. Foltz. Marburg, 1904 (= *Veröffentlichungen der Historischen Kommission für Hessen und Waldeck*).

Urkundenbuch der Stadt Goslar. Vol. 5. Rev. by G. Bode. Halle, 1922.

Urkundenbuch der Stadt Grimma und des Klosters Nimbschen. Rev. by L. Schmidt. Leipzig, 1895 (= *Codex diplomaticus Saxoniae Regiae* 2, 15).

Urkundenbuch der Stadt Halberstadt. Vol. 1. Rev. by G. Schmidt. Halle, 1878 (= *Geschichtsquellen der Provinz Sachsen*. Vol. 7).

Urkundenbuch der Stadt Jena und ihrer geistlichen Anstalten. Vol. 1 (1182–1405). Ed. by J. E. A. Martin. Jena, 1888 (= *Thüringische Geschichtsquellen*. New series, 3).

Urkundenbuch der Stadt Magdeburg. Rev. by G. Hertel. 3 vols. Halle, 1892–1896 (= *Geschichtsquellen der Provinz Sachsen und angrenzender Gebiete*. Vols. 26–28).

Urkundenbuch der Stadt Regensburg. Vol. 2 (1351 to 1378). Rev. by F. Bastian and J. Widmann.

Munich, 1956 (= *Monumenta Boica.* New series, vol. 8).

Urkundenbuch der Stadt Strassburg. Vol. 1. Rev. by W. Wiegand. Strasbourg, 1879.

Urkundenbuch der Stadt Stuttgart. Ed. by A. Rapp. Stuttgart, 1892 (= *Württembergische Geschichtsquellen.* Vol. 13).

Urkunden und Briefe des Stadtarchivs Mellingen bis zum Jahre 1550. Rev. by H. Rohr. Aarau, 1960 (= *Quellen zur Aargauischen Geschichte* 1).

Das Verfestungsbuch der Stadt Stralsund. Ed. by O. Francke. Halle, 1875 (= *Hansische Geschichtsquellen.* Vol. 1).

Wanderbüchlein des Johannes Butzbach genannt Piemontanus. Ed. by L. Hoffmann. Berlin, no date.

A. Wendgraf, 'Aus den Denkwürdigkeiten der Helene Kottanerin 1439–1440', in: *Ungarische Rundschau für historische und soziale Wissenschaften* (1914) 3.

Wie ein Mann ein fromm Weib soll machen. Mittelalterliche Lehren über Ehe und Haushalt. Ed. by M. Della-piazza. Frankfurt on Main, 1984 (= *Insel Taschenbuch 745*).

Das Wiener Neustädter Stadtrecht. Ed. by G. Winkler. Vienna, 1880.

Zwickauer Rechtsbuch. Ed. in collaboration with E. Planitz, rev. by G. Ulbrich. Weimar, 1941.

Bibliography

Only a selection of the available literature is given here. In the case of collected volumes, the overall title is given, that is, individual contributions are not listed separately.

Adenauer, G.: *Das Ehe- und Familienrecht im Mühlhäuser Reichsrechtsbuch.* (Doctoral thesis.) Bonn, 1963.

Albistur, M., and D. Armogathe: *Histoire du féminisme français du Moyen Age à nos jours.* Paris, 1977.

Alltag im Spätmittelalter. Ed. by H. Kühnel in collaboration with H. Hundsbichler. Graz, Vienna, 1984.

Arnold, K.: *Kind und Gesellschaft in Mittelalter und Renaissance. Beiträge und Texte zur Geschichte der Kindheit.* Paderborn, 1980.

Bardèche, M.: *Histoire des femmes.* Vol. 1. Paris, 1968.

Bastian, F.: 'Das Manual des Regensburger Kaufhauses Runtinger und die mittelalterliche Frauenfrage', in: *Jahrbücher für Nationalökonomie und Statistik, 115/1920*, pp. 385–442.

Beard, H. R.: *Woman as force in history. A study in traditions and relations.* Chapter 13: 'An Illustrated Bibliography'. New York, 1962, pp. 341–369.

Bec, C.: *Les marchands écrivains à Florence 1375–1434.* Paris, 1967.

Behagel, W.: *Gewerbliche Stellung der Frau im mittelalterlichen Köln.* Berlin, 1910.

Bernards, M.: *Speculum Virginum—Geistigkeit und Seelenleben der Frau im Hochmittelalter.* Cologne, Graz, 1955.

Blockmans-Delva, A.: 'Het vlaamse 15de Eeuwse liber trotula, een praktijkboek van en voor vroedvrouwen', in: *Farmaceutisch tijdschrift voor België 58* (1981) 5/6.

Blöcker, M.: 'Die Geschichte der Frauen: erlebt, erlitten, vergessen?', in: *Frau—Realität und Utopie.* Ed. by C. Köppel and R. Sommerauer. Zurich, 1984, pp. 123–146.

Boesch, H.: *Kinderleben in der deutschen Vergangenheit.* Leipzig, 1900 (= *Monographien zur deutschen Kulturgeschichte.* Vol. 5).

Bogucka, M.: *Das alte Danzig. Alltagsleben vom 15. bis 17. Jahrhundert.* Leipzig, 1980.

Brodmeier, B.: *Die Frau im Handwerk in historischer und moderner Sicht.* Münster, 1963 (= *Forschungsberichte aus dem Handwerk.* Vol. 9).

De Bruin, C. C., E. Persons, and A. G. Weiler: *Geert Grote en de moderne devotie.* 2nd ed. Deventer, Zutphen, 1985.

Bücher, K.: *Die Berufe der Stadt Frankfurt am Main im Mittelalter.* Leipzig, 1914 (= *Abhandlungen der Philologisch-historischen Klasse der Königlich-Sächsischen Gesellschaft der Wissenschaften.* Vol. 30, 3).

Bücher, K.: *Die Frauenfrage im Mittelalter.* Tübingen, 1910.

Burckhard, G.: *Die deutschen Hebammenordnungen von ihren ersten Anfängen bis auf die Neuzeit.* Leipzig, 1912 (= *Studien zur Geschichte des Hebammenwesens* I, 1).

Delva, A.: 'Vrouwengeneeskunde in Vlandern tijdens de late middeleuwen met mitgave van het Brugse Liber Trotula', in: *Vlaamse Historische Studies 2.* Bruges, 1983.

Demelius, H.: *Eheliches Güterrecht im spätmittelalterlichen Wien.* Vienna, 1970 (= *Österreichische Akademie der Wissenschaften, Philologisch-historische Klasse, Sitzungsberichte 265, Abhandlung 4*).

Dienst, H.: 'Männerarbeit—Frauenarbeit im Mittelalter', in: *Beiträge zur historischen Sozialkunde* (1981) 3, pp. 88–90.

Dienst, H.: 'Rollenaspekte von Männern und Frauen im Mittelalter in zeitgenössischer Theorie und Praxis', in: *Weiblichkeit oder Feminismus? Beiträge zur interdisziplinären Frauentagung Konstanz 1983.* Ed. by C. Opitz. Weingarten, 1984, pp. 137–158.

Diepgen, P.: *Frau und Frauenheilkunde in der Kultur des Mittelalters.* Stuttgart, 1963.

Doren, A.: *Die Florentiner Wolltuchindustrie vom 14. bis zum 16. Jahrhundert*. Stuttgart, 1901.

Doren, A.: *Das Florentiner Zunftwesen vom 14. bis zum 16. Jahrhundert*. Stuttgart, 1908.

Dronke, P.: *Women Writers of the Middle Ages. A Critical Study of Texts from Perpetua († 203) to Marguerite Porète († 1310)*. Cambridge etc., 1984.

Duby, G.: *Le chevalier, la femme et le prêtre. Le mariage dans la France féodale*. Paris, 1981.

Dübeck, I.: *Købekoner og konkurrence: studier over myndighets-og erhvervsrettens udvikling med stadigt henblick på kvinders historiske retstilling*. Copenhagen, 1978 (= *Skrifter fra det retsvidenskabelige Institut ved Københavns Universitet 19*).

Ellermeyer, J.: *Stade 1300–1399, Liegenschaften und Renten in Stadt und Land. Untersuchungen zur Wirtschafts- und Sozialstruktur einer Hansischen Landstadt im Spätmittelalter*. Stade, 1975.

Enders, L., and F. Beck: 'Zur Geschichte des Nonnenklosters in Prenzlau und seiner Überlieferung', in: *Jahrbuch für Geschichte des Feudalismus*. Vol. 8. Berlin, 1984, pp. 158–190.

Ennen, E.: 'Die Frau in der Landwirtschaft vom Mittelalter bis zur frühen Neuzeit', in: *Die Frau in der deutschen Wirtschaft*. Stuttgart, 1985 (= *Zeitschrift für Unternehmensgeschichte*. Supplement 35).

Ennen, E.: 'Die Frau in der mittelalterlichen Stadtgesellschaft Mitteleuropas', in: *Hansische Geschichtsblätter*. Vol. 100. 1980.

Ennen, E.: 'Die Frau im Mittelalter. Eine Forschungsaufgabe unserer Tage', in: *Kurtriersches Jahrbuch* 21 (1981).

Ennen, E.: *Frauen im Mittelalter*. Munich, 1984.

Erbstösser, M., and E. Werner: *Ideologische Probleme des mittelalterlichen Plebejertums. Die freigeistige Häresie und ihre Wurzeln*. Berlin, 1960.

Erbstösser, M.: *Ketzer im Mittelalter*. Leipzig, 1984.

Erichson, C., and K. Casey: 'Women in the Middle Ages. A Working Bibliography', in: *Medieval Studies*. Vol. XXXVIII. 1976.

Fabian, E.: 'Die Zwickauer Schulbrüderschaft (Fraternitas Scholarium)', in: *Mitteilungen des Altertumsvereins für Zwickau und Umgebung* (1891) 3.

Familie und Gesellschaftsstruktur. Materialien zu den sozio-ökonomischen Bedingungen von Familienformen. Ed. and introduced by H. Rosenbaum. Frankfurt on Main, 1974.

Felser, R.: *Herkunft und soziale Schichtung der Bürgerschaft obersteirischer Städte und Märkte unter besonderer Berücksichtigung der Bürger der Stadt Judenburg*. (Doctoral thesis at Graz University, 38.) Vienna, 1977.

La femme. Vol. 3. Brussels, 1962 (= *Recueils de la société Jean Bodin* 12).

'La femme dans les civilisations des Xe–XIIIe siècles. Actes du Colloque tenu à Poitiers les 23–25e Septembre 1976', in: *Cahiers de Civilisations Médiévales*. Vol. 20. 1977.

Frank, K. S.: *Das Klarissenkloster Söflingen. Ein Beitrag zur franziskanischen Ordensgeschichte Süddeutschlands und zur Ulmer Kirchengeschichte*. Ulm, 1980 (= *Forschungen zur Geschichte der Stadt Ulm*. Vol. 20).

Frau im spätmittelalterlichen Alltag. Vienna, 1986 (= *Veröffentlichungen des Instituts für Mittelalterliche Realienkunde Österreichs, Österreichische Akademie der Wissenschaften, Philosophisch-historische Klasse. Sitzungsberichte*. 473rd vol.).

Fritz, W. D.: 'Die Neuverleihung des Colmarer Stadtrechts an Kaysersberg, Münster und Türkheim im Jahre 1354', in: *Stadt- und Städtebürgertum in der deutschen Geschichte des 13. Jahrhunderts*. Ed. by B. Töpfer. Berlin, 1976, pp. 372–388 (= *Forschungen zur mittelalterlichen Geschichte*. Vol. 24).

Gerz von Büren, V.: *Geschichte des Clarissenklosters St. Clara in Kleinbasel 1266–1529.* Basle, 1969.

Gloger, B., and W. Zöllner: *Teufelsglauben und Hexenwahn.* Leipzig, 1983.

Gössmann, E.: *Die streitbaren Schwestern. Was will die feministische Theologie?* Freiburg im Breisgau, 1981 (= *Herderbücherei* 879).

Greer, G.: *Das unterdrückte Talent. Die Rolle der Frauen in der bildenden Kunst.* Berlin, Vienna, 1979.

Grimm, P.: 'Zwei bemerkenswerte Gebäude in der Pfalz Tilleda. Eine zweite Tuchmacherei', in: *Prähistorische Zeitschrift* (1963) 41.

Gross, C.: *The guild merchant—a contribution to British municipal history.* Vol. 1, 2. Oxford, 1964 (Reprint of the 1st ed. Oxford, 1890).

Grundmann, H.: *Religiöse Bewegungen im Mittelalter.* Hildesheim, 1961.

Händler-Lachmann, B.: 'Die Berufstätigkeit der Frau in den deutschen Städten des Spätmittelalters und der beginnenden Neuzeit', in: *Hessisches Jahrbuch für Landesgeschichte* 30. 1980.

Hagemann, H. R.: 'Basler Stadtrecht im Spätmittelalter', in: *Zeitschrift der Savigny-Stiftung für Rechtsgeschichte, Germanistische Abteilung* (1961) 78.

Harksen, S.: *Die Frau im Mittelalter.* Leipzig, 1974.

Hartwig, J.: 'Die Frauenfrage im mittelalterlichen Lübeck', in: *Hansische Geschichtsblätter* 14. 1908.

Haus und Familie in der spätmittelalterlichen Stadt. Ed. by A. Haverkamp. Cologne, Vienna, 1984 (= *Städteforschung.* Series A, vol. 18).

Herlihy, D.: 'Land, family and women in Continental Europe 700–1200', in: *Traditio* (1962) 18, pp. 89 to 120.

Herlihy, D.: *Woman in Medieval Society.* Houston, 1971 (= *The Smith History Lecture* 14).

Herlihy, D.: 'The medieval marriage market', in: *Medieval and Renaissance Studies* VI. 1976, pp. 3–27.

Herlihy, D., and C. Klapisch-Zuber: *Les Toscans et leurs familles. Une étude du Catasto florentin de 1427.* Paris, 1978.

Hess, L.: *Die deutschen Frauenberufe des Mittelalters.* Munich, 1940.

Histoire mondiale de la femme. Ed. by P. Grimal. Vol. 2. Paris, 1966.

Höher, F.: 'Hexe, Maria und Hausmutter. Zur Geschichte der Weiblichkeit im Spätmittelalter', in: *Frauen in der Geschichte.* Vol. 3. Ed. by A. Kuhn and J. Rüsen. Düsseldorf, 1983.

Hurd-Mead, K. C.: *A history of women in medicine.* Haddam, Conn., 1938.

Jaritz, G.: 'Österreichische Bürgertestamente als Quelle zur Erforschung städtischer Lebensformen des Spätmittelalters', in: *Jahrbuch für Geschichte des Feudalismus.* Vol. 8. Berlin, 1984, pp. 249–264.

Jastrebickaja, A. L.: 'Die Familie als soziale Gruppe der mittelalterlichen Gesellschaft', in: *Jahrbuch für Geschichte des Feudalismus.* Vol. 6. Berlin, 1982, pp. 185–193.

Jastrebickaja, A. L.: 'Über einige Gesichtspunkte der Familienstruktur und der Verwandtschaftsbeziehungen in der mittelalterlichen Stadt', in: *Jahrbuch für Geschichte des Feudalismus.* Vol. 8. Berlin, 1984, pp. 191–204.

Jehel, G.: 'Le rôle des femmes et du milieu familial à Gênes dans les activités commerciales au cours de la première moitié du XIIIᵉ siècle', in: *Revue d'histoire économique et sociale* (1975) 53, pp. 193ff.

Kaminsky, H. H.: 'Die Frau in Recht und Gesellschaft des Mittelalters', in: *Frauen in der Geschichte.* Vol. 1. Ed. by A. Kuhn and G. Schneider. Düsseldorf, 1979, pp. 295–313.

Ketsch, P.: 'Aspekte der rechtlichen und politisch-gesellschaftlichen Situation von Frauen im frühen Mittelalter (500–1150)', in: *Frauen in der Geschichte.* Vol. 2. Ed. by A. Kuhn and J. Rüsen. Düsseldorf, 1982, pp. 11–72.

Kirshner, J., and S. Wemple: *Women of the Medieval World*. Oxford, 1985.

Kleinbub, M.: *Das Recht der Übertragung und Verpfändung von Liegenschaften in der Reichsstadt Ulm bis 1548*. Ulm, 1961 (= *Forschungen zur Geschichte der Stadt Ulm*. Vol. 3).

Koch, G.: *Frauenfrage und Ketzertum im Mittelalter. Die Frauenbewegungen im Rahmen des Katharismus und des Waldensertums und ihre sozialen Wurzeln (12.–14. Jahrhundert)*. Berlin, 1962 (= *Forschungen zur mittelalterlichen Geschichte*. Vol. 9).

'Kongress "Frau und spätmittelalterlicher Alltag". Zusammenfassung', in: *Medium Aevum Quotidianum. Newsletter 4*. Krems, 1984.

Kotel'nikova, L. A.: 'Sel'skoe chozjajstvo na zemljach Strozzi—krupnoj popolanskoj semi Toskany XV v. (Po materialam Gosudarstvennogo archiva Florencii)', in: *Srednie Veka*. Moscow (1984) 47.

Kroemer, B.: 'Von Kauffrauen, Beamtinnen, Ärztinnen. Erwerbstätige Frauen in deutschen mittelalterlichen Städten', in: *Frauen in der Geschichte*. Vol. 2. Düsseldorf, 1982.

Kroeschell, K.: *Deutsche Rechtsgeschichte*. 2 vols. Hamburg, 1972–1983 (= *rororo studium 8–9*).

Kuehn, T.: 'Women, marriage and "patria potestas" in late medieval Florence', in: *Revue d'histoire du droit* (1981) 49, pp. 127–147.

Küttler, W.: 'Stadt und Bürgertum im Feudalismus. Zu theoretischen Problemen der Stadtgeschichtsforschung in der DDR', in: *Jahrbuch für Geschichte des Feudalismus*. Vol. 4. Berlin, 1980, pp. 75–112.

Lambert, E.: *Die Rathsgesetzgebung der freien Reichsstadt Mühlhausen in Thüringen im 14. Jahrhundert*. Halle, 1870.

Lambert, M.: *Ketzerei im Mittelalter. Häresien von Bogumil bis Hus*. Munich, 1981.

Lauterer-Pirner, H.: 'Vom "Frauenspiegel" zu Luthers Schrift "Vom ehelichen Leben". Das Bild der Ehefrau im Spiegel einiger Zeugnisse des 15. und 16. Jahrhun-

derts', in: *Frauen in der Geschichte*. Vol. 3. Düsseldorf, 1983, pp. 63–85.

Le Goff, J.: 'Petits enfants dans la littérature des XIIe–XIIIe siècles', in: *Annales de Démographie Historique*. 1973, pp. 129–132.

Lehmann, A.: *Le rôle de la femme dans l'histoire de France au Moyen Age*. Paris, 1952.

Lehnert, M.: 'Geoffrey Chaucer—Der Dichter der Liebe', in: *Realismus und literarische Kommunikation. Dem Wirken Rita Schobers gewidmet* (= *Sitzungsberichte der Akademie der Wissenschaften der DDR/Gesellschaftswissenschaften 8/G*). Berlin, 1984, pp. 61–77.

Leipoldt, J.: *Die Frau in der antiken Welt und im Urchristentum*. Leipzig, 1954.

Lendorff, G.: *Kleine Geschichte der Baslerin*. Basle, Stuttgart, 1966.

Lévy, J. P.: 'L'officialité de Paris et les questions familiales à la fin du XIVe siècle', in: *Études d'histoire du droit canonique dédiées à Gabriel Le Bras*. Vol. 2. Paris, 1965, pp. 1265–1294.

Loose, H. C.: 'Erwerbstätigkeit der Frau im Spiegel Lübecker und Hamburger Testamente', in: *Zeitschrift des Vereins für Lübeckische Geschichts- und Altertumskunde* 60. 1980, pp. 9–20.

Lorenzen-Schmidt, K. J.: 'Zur Stellung der Frauen in der frühneuzeitlichen Städtegesellschaft Schleswigs und Holsteins', in: *Archiv für Kulturgeschichte* 61. 1979, pp. 316–339.

Lüers, G.: *Die Sprache der deutschen Mystik des Mittelalters im Werke der Mechthild von Magdeburg*. Darmstadt, 1966.

Maertens, R.: *Wertorientierungen und wirtschaftliches Erfolgsstreben mittelalterlicher Grosskaufleute. Das Beispiel Gent im 13. Jahrhundert*. Cologne, Vienna, 1976 (= *Kollektive Einstellungen und sozialer Wandel im Mittelalter*. Ed. by R. Sprandel. Vol. 5).

Maschke, E.: 'Die Familie in der deutschen Stadt des späten Mittelalters', in: *Sitzungsberichte der Heidel-*

berger Akademie der Wissenschaften, Philosophisch-historische Klasse. Annual set 1980.

Mölk, U.: 'Die literarische Entdeckung der Stadt im französischen Mittelalter', in: *Über Bürger, Stadt und städtische Literatur im Spätmittelalter. Bericht über Kolloquien der Kommission zur Erforschung der Kultur des Spätmittelalters 1975–1977.* Ed. by J. Fleckenstein and K. Stackmann. Göttingen, 1980.

Mutschlechner, G.: 'Frauen als Bergbauunternehmer im ehemaligen Berggericht Sterzing', in: *Schlern. Zeitschrift für Heimat- und Volkskunde.* 37th annual set. Bozen, 1963.

Nicholas, D.: *The Domestic Life of a Medieval City-Woman. Children and the Family in Fourteenth-Century Ghent.* Lincoln, London, 1985.

Nübel, O.: *Mittelalterliche Beginen- und Sozialsied-lungen in den Niederlanden.* Tübingen, 1970.

Opitz, C.: *Frauenalltag im Mittelalter. Biographien des 13. und 14. Jahrhunderts.* Weinheim, Basle, 1985 (= *Ergebnisse der Frauenforschung.* Vol. 5).

Osterloh, J.: *Die Rechtsstellung der Handelsfrau.* (Doctoral thesis.) Eutin, 1919.

Quast, J.: 'Vrouwenarbeid omstreeks 1500 in enkele Nederlandse steden', in: *Jaarboek voor vrouwenge-schiedenis.* 1980, pp. 50–60.

Riemer, E. S.: *Women in the Medieval City. Sources and uses of wealth by Sienese women in the thirteenth century.* (Doctoral thesis.) New York, 1975.

The Role of Woman in the Middle Ages. Ed. by R. T. Morewedge. Albany, 1975.

Rüdiger, B.: 'Zur Reflexion der Frauenfrage in der deutschen Frauenmystik des 13./14. Jahrhunderts', in: *Untersuchungen zur gesellschaftlichen Stellung der Frau im Feudalismus.* Magdeburg, 1981 (= *Magdeburger Beiträge zur Stadtgeschichte.* No. 3).

Schildhauer, J.: 'Zur Lebensweise und Kultur der hansestädtischen Bevölkerung—auf der Grundlage der Stralsunder Bürgertestamente (Anfang 14. bis Ende 16. Jahrhundert)', in: *Wissenschaftliche Zeitschrift der Ernst-Moritz-Arndt-Universität Greifswald* (1981) 1/2.

Schmidt, G.: *Die berufstätige Frau in der Reichsstadt Nürnberg bis zum Ende des 16. Jahrhunderts.* Erlangen, 1950.

Schmoller, G.: *Die Strassburger Tucher- und Weber-zunft. Urkunden und Darstellung, nebst Regesten und Glossar. Ein Beitrag zur Geschichte der deutschen Weberei und des deutschen Gewerberechts vom 13.–17. Jahrhundert.* Strasbourg, 1879.

Schneider, A.: 'Frauen in den Flugschriften der frühen Reformationsbewegung', in: *Jahrbuch für Geschichte des Feudalismus.* Vol. 7. Berlin, 1983, pp. 247–264.

Schraut, E., and C. Opitz: *Frauen und Kunst im Mittelalter.* Exhibition catalogue. Brunswick, 1983.

Schubart-Fikentscher, G.: 'Das Brünner Schöffenbuch. Beiträge zur spätmittelalterlichen Rechts- und Kulturgeschichte', in: *Deutsches Archiv für Geschichte des Mittelalters* 1. 1937, pp. 457–498.

Schuchhardt, W.: *Weibliche Handwerkskunst im deutschen Mittelalter.* Berlin, 1941.

Schuler, T.: 'Familien im Mittelalter', in: *Die Familie in der Geschichte.* Ed. by H. Reif. Göttingen, 1982 (= *Kleine Vandenhoeck-Reihe* 1474).

Schuller, H.: 'Dos-Praebenda-Peculium', in: *Festschrift für F. Hausmann.* Ed. by H. Ebner. Graz, 1977, pp. 453–487.

Schultheiss, W.: *Die Münchner Gewerbeverfassung im Mittelalter.* Munich, 1936.

Schuster, D.: *Die Stellung der Frau in der Zunft-verfassung.* Berlin, 1927.

Shahar, S.: *Die Frau im Mittelalter.* Translated by R. Achlama. Königstein/Taunus, 1981.

Stam, S. M.: 'Die ökonomischen Grundlagen der Herausbildung und Entwicklung der mittelalterlichen Stadt in West- und Mitteleuropa', in: *Jahrbuch für Geschichte des Feudalismus*. Vol. 2. Berlin, 1978.

Stenton, M.D.: *The English Woman in History*. New York, 1977.

Trexler, R.D.: 'La prostitution florentine au XVe siècle. Review', in: *Annales. Economies, Sociétés, Civilisations*. Paris 38 (1981) 6.

Uitz, E.: 'Die Frau im Berufsleben der spätmittelalterlichen Stadt, untersucht am Beispiel von Städten auf dem Gebiet der Deutschen Demokratischen Republik', in: *Frau im spätmittelalterlichen Alltag*. Vienna, 1986, pp. 439–473 (= *Veröffentlichungen des Instituts für Mittelalterliche Realienkunde Österreichs, Österreichische Akademie der Wissenschaften, Philologisch-historische Klasse. Sitzungsberichte*. 473rd vol.).

Uitz, E.: 'Frau und gesellschaftlicher Fortschritt in der mittelalterlichen Stadt', in: *Zeitschrift für Geschichtswissenschaft* (1984) 12, pp. 1071–1083.

Uitz, E.: 'Zu einigen Aspekten der gesellschaftlichen Stellung der Frau in der mittelalterlichen Stadt', in: *Jahrbuch für Geschichte des Feudalismus*. Vol. 5. Berlin, 1981, pp. 57–88.

Uitz, E.: 'Zur Darstellung der Stadtbürgerin, ihrer Rolle in Ehe, Familie und Öffentlichkeit in der Chronistik und in den Rechtsquellen der spätmittelalterlichen deutschen Stadt', in: *Jahrbuch für Geschichte des Feudalismus*. Vol. 7. Berlin, 1983, pp. 130–156.

Uitz, E.: 'Zur gesellschaftlichen Stellung der Frau in der mittelalterlichen Stadt (Die Situation im Erzbistum Magdeburg)', in: *Magdeburger Beiträge zur Stadtgeschichte*. Magdeburg (1977) 1, pp. 20–42.

'Untersuchungen zur gesellschaftlichen Stellung der Frau im Feudalismus'. Ed. by Historikergesellschaft der Deutschen Demokratischen Republik, in: *Magdeburger Beiträge zur Stadtgeschichte*. Magdeburg (1981) 3.

Vetter, A.: *Bevölkerungselemente der ehemals Freien Reichsstadt Mühlhausen in Thüringen im XV. und XVI. Jahrhundert*. Leipzig, 1910 (= *Leipziger Historische Abhandlungen*. No. XVII).

Wachendorf, H.: *Die wirtschaftliche Stellung der Frau in den deutschen Städten des späten Mittelalters*. Hamburg, 1934.

Weber, M.: *Ehefrau und Mutter in der Rechtsentwicklung. Eine Einführung*. Tübingen, 1907.

Weber-Kellermann, I.: *Die deutsche Familie. Versuch einer Sozialgeschichte*. Frankfurt on Main, 1974.

Wensky, M.: 'Die Frau in Handel und Gewerbe vom Mittelalter bis zur frühen Neuzeit', in: *Die Frau in der deutschen Wirtschaft*. Stuttgart, 1985, pp. 30–44 (= *Zeitschrift für Unternehmensgeschichte*. Supplement 35).

Wensky, M.: *Die Stellung der Frau in der stadtkölnischen Wirtschaft im Spätmittelalter*. Cologne, Vienna, 1980 (= *Quellen und Darstellungen zur Hansischen Geschichte*. New series. Vol. XXVI).

Werner, E.: *Pauperes Christi*. Leipzig, 1956.

Werner, E.: 'Vita religiosa als vita humana einer aussergewöhnlichen Frau—Heloise mit und ohne Abaelard', in: *Realismus und literarische Kommunikation. Dem Wirken Rita Schobers gewidmet*. Berlin, 1984, pp. 52–60 (= *Sitzungsberichte der Akademie der Wissenschaften der DDR, Gesellschaftswissenschaften 8/G*).

Werner, E.: *Stadt und Geistesleben im Hochmittelalter. 11. bis 13. Jahrhundert*. Weimar, 1980 (= *Forschungen zur mittelalterlichen Geschichte*. Vol. 30).

Wesoly, K.: 'Der weibliche Bevölkerungsanteil in spätmittelalterlichen und frühneuzeitlichen Städten und die Betätigung von Frauen im zünftigen Handwerk (insbesondere am Mittel- und Oberrhein)', in: *Zeitschrift für die Geschichte des Oberrheins* 128. 1980, pp. 69–117.

Winter, A.: 'Studien zur sozialen Situation der Frauen in der Stadt Trier nach der Steuerliste von 1364. Die

Unterschicht', in: *Kurtriersches Jahrbuch* 15 (1975), pp. 20–45.

Winter, G.: *Das eheliche Güterrecht im älteren hamburgischen Recht. Dargestellt an Stadtbucheintragungen aus dem 13./14. Jahrhundert.* Hamburg, 1958.

Wolf-Graaf, A.: *Die verborgene Geschichte der Frauenarbeit. Eine Bildchronik.* Weinheim, Basle, 1983.

Wulff, A.: *Die frauenfeindlichen Dichtungen in der romanischen Literatur des Mittelalters bis zum Ende des 13. Jahrhunderts.* Halle, 1914 (= *Romanische Arbeiten* 4).

Aus der Zeit der Verzweiflung. Zur Genese und Aktualität des Hexenbildes. Published under the editorship of G. Busch, 2nd ed. Frankfurt on Main, 1978 (= *edition suhrkamp* 840).

Index of Names and Places

Sources of Illustrations

Illustrations in the text are
given with the respective page numbers;
all other figures refer to the numbers of
illustrations.

Klaus G. Beyer, Weimar 1, 26, 46, 47, 48, 62, 66, 68

Bibliothèque de l'Arsenal, Paris 20, 21

Bibliothèque Historique de la ville de Paris back endpaper

Bibliothèque Municipale, Orléans p. 105

Bibliothèque Nationale, Paris 16, 19, 28, 29, 31, 32, 33, 34, 44, 51

British Museum, London 63, 64, p. 107, p. 174

Church of the Virgin Mary, Parchim 56

Forschungsbibliothek Gotha 39

Herzog Anton Ulrich Museum, Brunswick p. 99

Institut für Denkmalspflege of the German Democratic Republic, Berlin 41

Institut für mittelalterliche Realienkunde Österreichs, Krems 4, 12, 22, 23, 24, 49, 50, 53, 54, 55, 61, 65, 70, 71

Rainer Kitte, Görlitz 69

Bertram Kober, Leipzig front endpaper p. 4, p. 8, p. 45, p. 65, p. 66, p. 101, p. 104, p. 106, p. 117, p. 147, p. 148, p. 169, p. 172

Württembergische Landesbibliothek, Stuttgart 58

Municipal and University Library, Berne 2, 3, 25, 27, 40

Municipal Library, Bruges p. 69

Museen der Stadt Gotha 42

Museum der bildenden Künste, Leipzig 18

Museum of Fine Arts, Budapest 43, 45, 67

Österreichische Nationalbibliothek, Vienna 6, 17, 52, 57, 59, p. 67, p. 68 below, p. 69 below, p. 70, p. 154, p. 155, p. 174 right

Joachim Petri, Mölkau near Leipzig p. 149, p. 150

Janusz Podlecki, Cracow 5, 14

Publisher's Archives 11, 13, 15

Rosgartenmuseum, Constance 8, 9

Schweizerisches Landesmuseum, Zurich 10

Staatliche Museen zu Berlin, Picture Gallery 7

Stadtarchiv Rostock 30

Stadtarchiv Stralsund 35, p. 115

Städtische Museen, Freiberg im Breisgau 60

Stadtmuseum, Graz 38

Stadt- und Kreisarchiv Mühlhausen/Thuringia p. 111, p. 112, p. 175

Stadt- und Kreisarchiv Zwickau 36, 37

Paris—residence of the French kings, university centre of western Europe in the late Middle Ages, and an important crossing point for long-distance trade—also had close links with the neighbouring countryside. The town created possibilities of work for many women.

Georg Braun, 'Plan of the City of Paris with Three People', from *Civitates orbis terrarum*. Cologne, 1576. Bibliothèque Historique de la Ville de Paris